The 100

Best Spare-Time Business Opportunities Today

KEVIN HARRINGTON
MARK N. COHEN

WILEY

John Wiley and Sons, Inc.
NEW YORK · CHICHESTER · BRISBANE ·
TORONTO · SINGAPORE

Dedicated to the countless
entrepreneurs who have cashed in
on the money to be made,
independence to be gained,
and fun to be had from
their own spare-time
business opportunity.

Library of Congress Cataloging-in-Publication Data:
Harrington, Kevin.
        The 100 best spare-time business opportunities today/Kevin
Harrington, Mark N. Cohen.
        p.   cm.
        ISBN 0-471-61134-4. -- ISBN 0-471-61133-6 (pbk.)
        1. New business enterprises--United States and Canada.
2.Entrepreneurship--United States and Canada.   I. Cohen,
Mark N.   II. Title.   III. Title : One hundred best spare-time
business opportunities today.
HD62.5.H3735   1990
338.7'4'02573--dc20   89-22765
                                                                CIP

Printed in the United States of America

90 91 10 9 8 7 6 5 4 3 2 1

CONTENTS

INTRODUCTION

The following are trademarks, registered names or proprietary brand names of the companies listed in this book.

AIR-serv Tire Inflator
Badge-A-Minit
Bi-Weekly Mortgage
    Reduction
Bi-Weekly Presentation
Black Magic Pressure
    Washing
Chains-by-the-Inch
Closet Space Savers
Colortech System 1000
Communidyne Model 2000
Dip-er-do
Donut Man Machine
Dry Foam Extraction System
Dry Foam Upholstery
    Extractor System
Electrostatic Air Filters
Executive Etiquette Start-Up
    Package
Fabulous Mouli-M2 French
    Processor
Fabulous Wok of China
Ginsu Knives
Gold Card
Granular Activated Carbon
    Systems

Homestead Publications
Hydrocote
MasterCard
Odor Kill
Our Secret Creations
Pepsi-Cola
Personal Service Company
Picturegraphics
Power Wall Cleaning System
Seamless Spray
Soot Set
Soot Sweeper
Special-T Porclynite
Stolichnaya
Talking Balloon
Telehelp Service
The Blade
The Magical Cleaning Cloth
Trump Card
Ultra Violet Absorbing Agent
    2.2, Di-H-4M
Video Magalog
VISA
World of Winners

INTRODUCTION

So You Want to Start Your Own Spare-Time Business

Welcome to the wonderful world of excitement, challenge, fun, and increased income with your own spare-time business opportunity!

This book can change your life. It has been written to maximize your earning power by introducing you to the 100 best money-making opportunities for the 1990s. You're about to learn 100 ways to earn extra money: new ways, proven ways, surefire ways—even ingenious ways to put your earning power into fast gear.

Spare-time businesses seem to be part of today's work ethic. They enable you to make ends meet whether or not you have a full-time job; they patch up financial shortages and generate cash for whatever reason you may need a few extra dollars. And most people can think of several reasons.

One of the prime benefits of your own spare-time business is its flexibility. More and more people are earning their entire living without any semblance of a full-time job. All their income comes from side ventures. Of course, many of the opportunities you'll learn about in this guide can be a full-time business, earning you even more money. Still, most people who will read this book hold down full-time jobs, or are students or homemakers, but want to supplement their income by moonlighting in their own entrepreneurial side ventures. In fact, over 30 percent of all income comes from part-time business ventures. This gives you some idea of their growing acceptance and popularity.

If you now hold a full-time job, you'll discover that a spare-time business can easily be tailored to fit your exact work and life situation. It allows you to make additional money and is easily accomplished in your spare time, making little if any demands on your full-time commitments. As your spare-time venture proves successful, you can easily expand it to a full-time money maker. That's why so many people, like you, are so interested in spare-time opportunities. Instead of requiring you to work set hours and set days, a spare-time business allows you to work only when it is convenient for you to work. Instead of providing you with a set income, your own spare-time enterprise offers a flexible income, limited only by the time and effort you choose to expend.

Another favorable characteristic of a spare-time business is that it enables you to fit into your community more fully and directly. As you look over the 100 methods we present for earning extra income, you'll agree there is a real need for these services or products right where you live. As you consider each opportunity, ask yourself whether this type business would be welcomed in your community. Many part-time entrepreneurs have found their service or product is very much appreciated by the people right in their own neighborhood, and this often offers a great opportunity to make more friends and develop new relationships. This alone may offer sufficient incentive. The people you meet and work with in your new venture can, indeed, fill your extra money-making hours with fun and enjoyment.

Don't delay! These are ideal times to start your own spare-time business. Things are going exceptionally well for people with spare-time ventures these days. The number of part-time operations keeps growing—and for plenty of good reasons. Why?

1. *More demand for creativity and newness.* People are demanding more creativity and novelty in what they buy. Research shows that small businesses and spare-time opportunities produce the majority of the innovations in our country. In fact, they produce 24 times more innovations per dollar of development money than the big companies do.

   As big businesses grow bigger, former risk-taking entrepreneurs turn to cumbersome procedures that stifle creativity. This means creativity will be in big demand and your business will most likely be on the cutting edge of that creativity.

2. *More opportunities.* Uncertain times cause problems both for consumers and for large corporations. But they offer new opportunities for those best at solving problems: small and part-time businesses.

There are many problems for which new and spare-time companies can profitably develop solutions at a far greater rate than do large companies. Here are just a few:

- Greater productivity
- Less-expensive products and services
- Higher-quality products that last longer
- More-convenient entertainment
- Better repair services
- Training for new careers or better employee performance
- Services to the growing number of affluent elderly
- Solutions to health care problems.

Once you begin to read about the opportunities in this book, you'll see just what is meant.

3. *Rising demand for specialization and quality*. People no longer want the same products and services as everyone else. Increasingly, they buy what serves their particular pocketbook, tastes, needs, and ethnic background.

For example, ten years ago the average supermarket had 9,000 different items. Now there are over 22,000. And consumers demand still more specialization. This trend toward serving small groups of customers and fewer mass markets gives you a big advantage over large firms.

When you check our 100 opportunities, you will discover quality and specialization to niche markets is the strength they are built on.

4. *Rising demand for services*. Over half of our consumer expenditures are for services. In the last period of economic downturn, service expenditures still grew by nearly 5 percent, whereas sales of goods declined nearly 3 percent. This year, growth of 10 percent or more is expected for many service industries.

Moreover, businesses are increasingly turning to subcontractors to supply needed services with greater flexibility and at lower cost. And busy, multi-income families can scarcely find enough services to help ease their time pressures.

Also, small service companies have an advantage over large ones because local owners can ensure the personal attention consumers are willing to pay for. In short, by creating convenience for somebody else, you can make money for yourself. Because of these trends, many spare-time opportunities are created every day to capitalize on today's exploding need for service businesses.

5. *More respect everywhere.* Let's face it, until recently, bankers, suppliers, and potential employees often ignored—even shunned—spare-time business. Big companies were the heroes of our economy; they had stability, success, and professionalism.

Today the spotlight is on the small company and spare-time business because their numbers are growing much faster than the giants.

Firms of every size have found that small businesses are an excellent market today, and they will be out to get you as a customer. You may have seen ads directed to small-business owners by phone companies, computer firms, banks, and other financial institutions that a few years ago had little interest in dealing with small business.

Even employees are more plentiful for the spare-time business. Within the past five years, more than 5 million people with three or more years' experience were let go. Added to this are countless students, homemakers, and even full-time employees looking to moonlight. That means that a lot of highly qualified people will be eager to work for you.

What all this means is that years ago there were fewer successful spare-time ventures, and a new start-up had fewer people to turn to when it needed help and advice. That has all changed now that spare-time enterprises have become the fastest growing segment of the U.S. economy.

Most importantly, there are thousands of successful spare-time operators who are ready to share their success with you. So you can now share the ideas, concepts, and experiences of these proven money makers. As you follow their lead, you avoid the research costs and costly mistakes of journeying into business on your own. Read on. The *100 Best* featured here will prove to you that these are indeed the best times to make big money in your own spare-time business.

Why These Are the Top 100

Researching the literally thousands of spare-time opportunities available today made it quite a challenge to pick what we considered to be the "100 best." What were those special characteristics that set the opportunities portrayed in this book apart from the rest—particularly when there were so many exciting money-making concepts to choose from?

To be in the running as a "best" business featured in this book, an offered opportunity had to stand out on four points:

- Income potential
- Fun
- Ease of entry and operation
- Stability.

So Who Wants to Be Wealthy?

If you have your sights on earning *top* dollar for every hour you spend with your business, then this book has the deals for you. Take Mark Saber, who now has his own tutoring service under *Top Marks Learning Network* banner and boasts a $900-a-week income on less than five hours' work. Those are the kind of opportunities we were looking for.

With such examples to lead the way, we scoured for deals profitable enough to put plenty of real money into your pocket—far more than you could earn working for a boss; and yes, even more than you might make slaving all day in a traditional full-time business.

Yet, this book doesn't promise you millions. The facts are that you *can* accumulate great wealth with just about any of the 100 exciting concepts featured. We heard of scores of opportunity seekers who have expanded nationwide or into full-time ventures, where millions were made from the businesses you'll learn about.

It's Gotta Be Fun

Typically, the people who have invested in one of these 100 best say they are "having a ball" because they were doing precisely the type of work they most enjoy. Yes, the 100 businesses you'll learn about can indeed be fun (or glamorous, stimulating, or creative). Many are fun simply because they are very different from the hum-drum businesses we come across every day. There are opportunities for people who like to sell, paint a ceiling, turn a wrench, or run a party. The objective was to pick the best from the broad gamut of opportunities available today. So whether you are hawking popcorn at an airport or helping college students find tuition money, there's a business to cater to every taste and talent.

It's So Easy

Starting your own spare-time business shouldn't mean you have to drain your life's savings or mortgage your house to raise thousands of dollars. Nor should you have to spend months to start. You want a business you can start on a proverbial "shoe-string," one that's easy to learn and simple to run. And that's what we found for you. You can even put yourself into scores of great businesses for under $1,000! With a great many of the opportunities shown here, you can recoup your investment in less than a week's time. But even the more expensive opportunities have price tags a fraction of what it would cost you to set up a comparable operation on your own.

With each of the opportunities presented, you receive everything you need to start so you can be in business right away. Most programs are simple to follow and need no special skills, education, or experience to operate. Whatever training or guidance you need is provided, whether in person or through manuals or videotape. Picking the best means we thoroughly checked to make sure you receive the support needed to guarantee your success.

Here Today, Here Tomorrow

Perhaps the greatest challenge was to find not only new, and unique businesses, but also those that had staying power. So plenty of fads were turned down that would be here today and gone tomorrow; only those we believe will stay in demand earning money for you year after year were selected. Many of the featured companies already enjoy a long track record, so they have proven stability. But, you'll agree, even the relatively new opportunities promise a concept that can only grow with time.

But What Business Is for Me?

Are you confused about the type of business you want?

Many people aren't really sure what business is best to start—all they do know is that they want their own spare-time business and the fun, opportunity, income, and challenge that only can come from being your own boss.

So how *do* you decide what business is best for you? First, read and carefully compare each of the opportunities presented in the pages that follow. Keep an open mind. Then ask yourself five tough questions:

1. What type of business do you think you would most enjoy?
2. What type of business requires the skills that most closely match your interests, aptitudes, training, or experience?
3. What type of business gives you the flexibility you need in terms of hours or supervision?
4. What type of business offers the expansion possibilities you may seek—the opportunity to become a full-time business or even a multi-unit enterprise?
5. What type of business can you most easily afford?

You see the idea. Try to develop a match between what you require from the business and, in turn, what you can offer the business. Once you have narrowed your focus, call or write the companies of interest for further information. These companies will, of course, tell you far more about their opportunity than can be provided within a few pages. Investigate each opportunity carefully. Talk to people who have purchased their opportunity. How satisfied are they? Does the company deliver on its promise? What are these people's earnings? How many hours do they work? What are the strengths and weaknesses of the business? Is the business growing? Perhaps you can get a better feel for the business by first working for someone in the business. Then you can see firsthand whether it's the one for you.

Whatever opportunity you choose, we sincerely wish you good luck in your new spare-time venture!

SCHOLARSHIP MATCHING / Academic Guidance Services, Inc.

Did you know that over $140 million of college financial aid went unclaimed last year? It's true. Thousands of scholarships and grants go unclaimed every year because students just don't know where to find financial help. This common problem opens up a highly unusual and rewarding opportunity for you to become a professional independent academic counselor. As part of the Academic Guidance Services team, you will be able to help students find the financial aid they so desperately need and be highly compensated for your efforts.

As an academic counselor, you will work closely with Academic Guidance Services, Inc. This is a nationwide electronic research organization that has developed and refined a unique and much-needed financial matching service. You work directly with students. (You never run out of prospects in this business!) They simply complete a short questionnaire so that their background and other information may be matched to the requirements of the funding sources and scholarships. Academic Guidance Services, in turn, guarantees to match a minimum of six financial sources to which the student is nominally qualified (or they will refund the processing fee and mail your student whatever sources were available). Practically all students can and do qualify for many forms of financial aid, so refunds are rare. You help these students attend college and at the same time earn a surprisingly high income. Where can you find a better opportunity?

All this has led to a growing number of profitable, independently owned businesses. Call it a student financial service or a scholarship matching service—it all adds up to a needed and wanted service in which you can help deserving students. Operate from your home or office, work full-time or spare-time. With the computerized assistance you'll receive from Academic Guidance Services, you step into a prestigious business that easily can be operated anywhere in the country.

The program is designed to fill a critical need of students. Fees are paid in advance directly to you, so there are never any credit problems. Practically no inventory (except some forms) is required. Processing is done by computer at Academic Guidance Services and is quickly back in your hands. No employees are necessary. No special skills are required and no personal sales are necessary. You set your own pace and you get your business going full blast quickly. There are no quotas to meet and no territorial restrictions to limit you. And, best of all, this service is always in demand and is not seasonal. In fact, owing to slashes in student aid and sky-rocketing increases in tuition costs, this business is now better than ever!

Here is what some academic counselors have to say about their association with Academic Guidance Services, Inc.: "This is by far the finest business-oriented program I have ever come across. With this type of support and background, there is no reason why anyone entering the program should not be successful." Another writes, "It seems our local newspaper published an article regarding the high cost of college and pointed out possible financial aid programs. They mentioned my company and gave the phone number. I received over 50 phone calls today." Still another writes, "I've been in the education field for over 20 years and believe me, Academic Guidance Services is great! I'm excited about the limitless possibilities and potential."

You can earn $50 or more on every student application submitted to Academic Guidance Services for processing (you set your fee), and since it only takes a few moments to complete each application, you can process applications nearly as fast as students can hand you their fee.

Students swarm to you once they know of your service—and you can reach the student market in so many different ways that they are impossible to list.

The cost of getting started in this field is low (only $495), with high rewards. There are no franchise fees or other costs except for the small per-application processing fee of less than

$20. If you want a business that offers both profits and prestige, consider scholarship matching.

For more information, write to

Academic Guidance Services, Inc.
15000 R Commerce Parkway
Mt. Laurel, NJ   08054-1015
(609) 727-1700

AIR DUCT CLEANING / Air-Care

Who would ever think a fortune could be lurking in those air duct systems found in just about every home, office, and commercial building?

But the fact is that dust aggravates breathing problems, causes burning eyes and itching skin, and worsens allergy problems. Health agencies, doctors, and scientific researchers claim that airborne dust may be one of the worst causes of health-related problems. Common house dust is far more dangerous to your health than outdoor dust. And that's why it is not only so nasty, but also *so* profitable. Once people realize that mounds of hazardous dust hide in their duct systems, they are glad to pay someone to clean their duct systems so they can breathe dust-free air again.

As a trained Air-Care technician, you are provided all the equipment you need to do the job professionally, efficiently, and profitably. Using Air-Care technical skills, you carefully remove the return registers and supply vents and vacuum inside the ducts as far as possible with a powerful HEPA-type vacuum.

Vents are thoroughly cleaned and washed and then temporarily covered with a special filter material and replaced into openings.

The Air-Care equipment then fogs a fine mist of Air-Care's special Soot Set sealer throughout the entire air duct system. Soot Set sealer cleans and refinishes the interior surface of the air duct system, making it like new. The main heating and cooling system is thoroughly cleaned, including the motor, case, and fan. This entire area is also fogged with Soot Set sealer. You then turn on the main ventilation system and Soot Set sealer and Solid Odor Kill deodorant fogs the entire system and assures complete coverage. The special temporary filters are removed from the vents and Solid Odor Kill deodorant blocks are placed into return registers. Finally, you install new, optional Electrostatic Air Filters. Available only from Air-Care, they are eleven times more efficient than disposable filters, and guaranteed for five years.

The demand for this unique service is so great that you can earn several hundred dollars a week working only on weekends. The cost to start is only $12,500. Air-Care provides the basic equipment, supplies, marketing material, and all the training you need.

One strong feature of Air-Care is its repeat business as customers call you for recleaning. This helps keep marketing costs low and profits high. Equally important, you confidently offer your community a vitally needed (and little-known) service to help protect their health.

Air-Care is not a franchise. There are no royalties to pay, and all the profits are yours. Air-Care is a solid growth business. No, it's not a "get rich quick" scheme, but a true opportunity to build a competition-free business in record time.

Air-Care operators report they can sell 20 to 30 percent of their targeted accounts. Yet this translates into considerable income, as you can earn $50 or more per hour with the Air-Care system. And it's a perfect spare-time business because customers prefer to be serviced during evenings and weekends so the service will not disrupt their operations.

Consider the vast market for this vitally needed service and you can see why it's one of our top 100!

For more information, write to

Air-Care Air Duct Decontamination Division
D.P.L. Enterprises, Inc.
5115 S. Industrial Road, Suite 506
Las Vegas, NV   89118
(800) 322-9919
In Nevada: (702) 736-4063

AIR-SERV TIRE INFLATORS / AIR-vend, Inc.

Remember the good old days when you could pull in to a gas station and fill your tires with *free* air? Forget it, those days are gone. Today "air" is the most profitable item a gas station sells.

AIR-vend, Inc. pioneered the development of the coin-operated tire inflator "AIR-serv" that is in wide use today in convenience stores and service stations throughout the United States, Canada, and Europe.

It was inevitable. Changes in the oil industry led to the birth of AIR-vend, Inc. As a result of higher gasoline prices and reduced service station profits, the nation's independent service station owners began looking for ways to cut corners. As mom-and-pop stations closed, oil jobbers began to convert these facilities to self-serve operations while adding convenience stores. Overhead was further reduced by employing only a single attendant or cashier.

The standard air compressor, long a key fixture of the service station, was suddenly a millstone: too cumbersome for the new format, too expensive to maintain, too bothersome for a single employee to operate.

Dave Bobert, president and founder of AIR-vend, Inc., started the company on the premise that nothing is free anymore. He says, "The trend is clear. Free air is going the way of the free road map. People may resent putting out a quarter, but [they] should realize they were always paying for the service. The cost of free air was just absorbed in the price paid for gas."

AIR-vend's AIR-serv Tire Inflators are coin-operated devices that produce their own compressed air. Each machine provides three and a half minutes' worth of air for 25 cents, and has a pressure gauge to measure the user's tire pressure.

6

AIR-serv Tire Inflators are marketed through a network of distributors in the United States, Canada, and Europe. The market potential includes over 200,000 locations. Although the major markets for these money-making machines have been service stations and convenience stores, wherever there are automobiles there is an installation opportunity.

When AIR-vend, Inc. was founded in 1981, fewer than 50 percent of all gas-selling locations were self-serve. By 1986, that number had risen to 78 percent. In that short period of time, the public completely changed its gas buying habits. At the same time, we have seen an enormous increase in the number of convenience stores—and many have added gas pumps. These two factors have produced a climate that is ripe for AIR-serv. AIR-vend currently has 40,000 AIR-serv units in operation, with room for thousands more.

To become an AIR-serv distributor, strong sales ambition is required, along with some business background. AIR-serv distributors operate independently. They buy machines from AIR-vend, Inc. and either sell them outright or place them on a share-the-revenue basis with the location owners.

Because distributors are the lifeline between the company and its customers, AIR-vend does not skimp on sales aids, training, or support. In addition to brochures, survey forms, spec sheets, trade shows, and informative newsletters; AIR-vend offers cooperative advertising programs featured in regional trade magazines.

Your return on investment is recouped in approximately 12 months. Each machine generates between $50 and $400 a month in revenue. Expenses for a typical machine run about $12.50 a month, and the location owner gets between 10 and 50 percent of the gross. (The average is 30–40 percent per machine.) Monthly net profit would be approximately $70.83 per unit based on the above scenario. A distributor with a multiple-unit route can easily earn in the six-figure range. The cost to start is between $15,000 and $60,000, depending on the number of units.

AIR-serv Tire Inflators are low-maintenance units that are available to serve the public's air needs 24 hours a day.

A typical distributor with 100 machines would spend approximately four days a month servicing his or her route since the equipment is relatively maintenance-free.

Entrepreneurs and retirees alike are jumping at the profit

potential of owning an AIR-serv coin-operated tire inflator business because profits are so attractive. AIR-serv installations have risen rapidly from none to more than 40,000 in just a few short years. And the low maintenance AIR-serv units are now welcome in service stations and convenience stores on a share-the-revenue basis. The more units a distributor owns, the more money is earned. There are no royalties, franchise fees, overhead, or restockable inventory.

Also, AIR-vend, Inc. now offers a complete line of AIR-serv products including tire inflators, air and water equipment, vacuums, vacuum and air combination units, heavy-duty tire inflators for trucks, and complimentary air. This boosts your profit potential even more!

AIR-vend can be like an annuity. Once a machine is installed, it will keep paying dividends year after year.

For more information, write to

AIR-vend, Inc.
1370 Mendota Heights Road
Mendota Heights, MN   55120
(800) 247-8363
In MN: (612) 454-0465
Contact: Dave Bobert, President, or
Doug Ascher, Marketing Director

LOW-COST SECURITY SYSTEMS / Alert Companion, Inc.

Did you know that nearly 6 million residential burglaries occurred last year? Did you know one of 14 households will be burglarized *this* year?

Now, at last, we found a very low cost but exceptionally effective security system that not only keeps burglars away, but can make a bundle for people selling this remarkable system to the estimated 40 million households that have absolutely no burglary protection whatsoever.

Alert Companion is a company that sells a unique state-of-the-art wireless security system with enormous potential. The system consists of a base station that protects vulnerable points of entry of the customer's premises. In addition to providing door and window protection, it also offers fire protection, panic buttons, gas detectors, motion detectors, and medical pendants. The components of the system are so vastly superior to others in the marketplace that many governmental buildings now use only Alert Companion. In fact, this is the smoke detector used in the West Wing of the White House. The system is portable, expandable, wireless, reliable, and extremely affordable. The Alert Companion system is beneficial for renters and apartment dwellers as well as homeowners. And it can be easily disconnected and removed from the premises with no damage when the customer moves, so the customer does not lose his or her investment. Since the system is modular, additional components can be purchased at a later date. Most importantly, the Alert Companion system is user-friendly. Customers can thus have fewer service calls and in turn save money. Every system is connected to a Central Emergency Monitoring Station on call to handle emergencies a full 365 days a year, 7 days a week, 24 hours a day. A half-hour video recently has been produced to attract dealers to the Alert Companion product, and a dealer manual explaining the Alert Companion business is sold through this video program.

The Alert Companion is a business opportunity for almost everyone. The market is vast! The video production focuses on attracting dealers who wish to supplement their income on a part-time basis. Alert Companion's video focuses on signing up dealers from city dwellers to suburban homeowners, men and women, retirees and college students. Virtually anybody who wishes to make big money is a good candidate for the Alert Companion business opportunity. Since crime is on the rise, the market is continually growing. The Alert Companion security system sells itself. People are interested in protecting their loved ones and personal property with a minimal investment, so there is a welcome smile when you show up with the Alert Companion to solve security problems efficiently and economically.

No special skills are required for this business opportunity. Alert Companion asks that you read the business manual and understand the general outline of the Alert Companion security system. There is a support staff in the main offices to answer any questions a dealer may have, and full marketing and technical support are offered to guarantee the success of serious representatives.

How much can you earn? You may not strike it rich, but you can earn a steady $10,000–$15,000 a year selling this system only 5–10 hours a week. But that works out to $30–$40 an hour, which probably beats your present full-time salary. Best of all, you can get started in this lucrative business for only $39.95 for a sample kit (less than the price of a good meal in a fancy restaurant).

Check out the Alert Companion for yourself and you'll see why we selected this as one of the hottest sideline opportunities of the year. Not only will you profit from the sale of the system, but you also make money from installations and, of course, enjoy continuous income from monitoring each system sold.

For more information, write to

Alert Companion, Inc.
162-30 Powells Cove Boulevard
Whitestone, NY   11357
(718) 767-0551

HOME-INSPECTION SERVICES / AmeriSpec, Inc.

Buying a home is considered the single largest purchase a person will make in a lifetime. But the American dream of home ownership too often becomes a horror story for buyers who fail to verify that the house they plan to purchase is in proper condition.

To help avert disaster, home shoppers are turning to home-inspection services in record numbers. Roy Cox, founder and president of AmeriSpec, Inc., a new franchised home-inspection service based in Orange, California, states, "The market is vast and expanding rapidly."

According to Cox, 3 million real estate transactions take place each year, but only 750,000 of those homes undergo inspection. "There is tremendous potential in this field. An average home today costs $100,000. The average inspection runs about $200. That's a small amount for a homeowner to invest for complete peace of mind," said Cox.

The home-inspection business is expanding so rapidly that Cox predicts it could grow to a $500–$600 million industry by the early 1990s.

"Just about anyone can learn to become a home inspector. There are no special skills required. It doesn't hurt to be handy around a home, but it is not a necessary prerequisite. The primary qualification is to be marketing oriented, because each franchise has to get out into the marketplace and sell its service."

The AmeriSpec franchise program includes an intensive two-week instruction course in professional home inspection, qualifying franchisees to conduct examinations of structural elements, roofing, foundations, plumbing, electrical wiring, heating and air conditioning systems, plus methods of checking

11

soil conditions that might contribute to wall and floor damage due to the settling of unstable ground.

"Franchisees will also be thoroughly trained in sales presentation techniques, business management and customer relations," said Cox.

The AmeriSpec franchise is designed both for individuals who want to be in a new business for themselves and for people currently in related fields, such as real estate, construction, escrow companies, home improvement, and property management.

An AmeriSpec franchise can be a full-time or spare-time business or a highly profitable division of a related existing business.

The franchise costs range from $12,500 to $17,500, which includes training, start-up assistance, marketing support, and consultation services. The royalty is 7 percent of gross sales and the advertising fee is 3 percent of gross sales.

Home inspection is an exploding industry, due in part to recent legislation requiring such inspections. We think AmeriSpec represents the kind of company that can best help you capture your share of this lucrative market.

We recommend AmeriSpec because it is the one company that provides the professional training that can turn anyone— with any background—into a top-notch home inspector delivering a much-needed service. And it's a service that can put as much as $100 an hour into *your* pocket!

For more information, write to

AmeriSpec, Inc.
1507 West Yale
Orange, CA   92667
(714) 998-2442
(800) 426-2270

FURNITURE RESTORATION /
Amity Quality Restoration Systems

Amity revolutionized the furniture-restoration industry by introducing the first completely nonflammable stripping system. This is the system that dramatically increased the volume of stripping possible, yet it attains a degree of quality never before achieved using older techniques.

Since the Amity system was first introduced in 1971, the restoration industry has grown tremendously. So has the Amity family of quality restoration centers. New shops have been opening at the rate of about one a week since that time. From Maine to California, craftsmen and -women have discovered the unsurpassed capabilities of the Amity system.

Many factors have contributed to this extraordinary growth. Amity continually stays abreast of innovations in the restoration field. The firm has spent years developing fast-acting yet safe nonflammable stripping chemicals that will not harm delicate wood fibers. This technology has established Amity as the choice of antique dealers and the nation's number one quality stripping and restoration system.

Safety *is* number one with Amity. Amity's Hydrocote brand water-based finishes eliminate the need for costly spray booths and reduce your operating insurance costs 40 to 60 percent over those of similar restoration shops using flammable lacquers and finishes. Hydrocote is nonflammable, noncombustible, and odorless. For you as a shop owner, this means you can operate your business in most any location without the restrictions placed on restoration shops using flammable lacquers.

13

The Amity system is more than high-quality chemicals and equipment. The training program, included in the system price, offers you complete professional instruction by experts in the field. The Amity system is an easy-to-use, commonsense method of restoration. Men and women are equally successful in this high-profit, low-overhead business, operating both part-time and full-time shops. Its versatility gives you the opportunity to tailor the business to your special area of interest, whether it be refinishing, restoration, sales, upholstering, or auctioneering. Using the Amity system, you can build a successful, full-service stripping and restoration business with no prior knowledge of the field. No special skills are required and labor is light.

Amity's professional staff are experienced and capable of assisting you with any stripping or restoration problem you may encounter. Service is the key to any restoration shop. Amity is the "Personal Service Company," which is the reason it was selected as one of the *100 Best*. Part-time earnings can be spectacular in this business, and start-up costs are surprisingly low. Many Amity dealers gross $4,000–$5,000 a week, and since overhead is relatively low, profits are correspondingly high. There is flexibility in what your start-up package may include, allowing you to increase your commitment to the business over time. Amity can tailor a business plan to your specific objectives.

Furniture restoration is a stable business. Sales and profits are consistent. Amity furnishes a strong marketing program, so your shop is likely to be appreciably more successful than your competition.

For more information, write to

**Amity Quality Restoration Systems
Box 7204
Madison, WI   53707
(608) 221-3585
(800) 334-4259**

HOROSCOPE DISPLAYS / Astrascope Corp.

Believe it or not, the National Science Foundation recently discovered that nearly two-thirds of all Americans occasionally read astrology, and a surprisingly large number anxiously read their horoscope every single day. Whether you are an astrology buff or not, we bet you too can hardly resist a peek at your own horoscope when you come across it.

Astrology is big business and it's growing bigger all the time. An estimated 35 million Americans are confirmed horoscope buffs. That's why Astrascope distributors sell millions of Astrascopes each and every year—and why Astrascope sales have increased more than fivefold in the past five years.

Astrascope publishes monthly horoscope scrolls sold through independent distributors to drug, convenience, and variety stores. An Astrascope distributor builds his or her business by asking store managers to place the Astrascope display on the checkout counters of their stores. The distributor enjoys a wide profit on sales from each display month after month for years on end.

Unlike most programs for distributors, Astrascope draws repeat sales. This sales base provides steady, sizable income while allowing the distributor to tailor his or her hours and income to his or her own needs. The distributor pays only for inventory. There are no hidden costs. In sum, an Astrascope distributorship can provide you a steady monthly income, flexible hours, and a great business of your own.

The limit of an Astrascope distributor's income hasn't been approached. There are distributors who only six months after starting with the program have built their business to an annual income in excess of $50,000.

What you earn, of course, depends largely on how many hours a week you wish to work. For example, a distributor servicing about 200 displays needs only eight to ten days each month to cover his or her route. This leaves the rest of the month to prospect for new accounts, take on additional product lines, or do whatever you like.

Each display measures only 5" × 6" (so merchants won't hesitate to place it in high-traffic areas) and holds $56.88 in merchandise—merchandise that turns 12 times a year on average. So you make several times your money month after month with each display.

No special skills, education, or experience is needed. Astrascope provides a distributor's manual as a guide, as well as continuous advice and guidance by phone.

You start your Astrascope distributorship for only $200 for inventory. But you can order a sample and other distributor information absolutely free.

Astrascope is a low-pressure business. Retailers welcome the line because it is so profitable and has a rapid turnover. Although we know of no Astrascope distributors who have become millionaires, we endorse this product line because it gives you clean, fast, and profitable sales with minimum hassle. And that's precisely the opportunity many people are looking for!

For more information, write to

Astrascope Corp.
78 Stone Place
Melrose, MA   02167
(617) 665-6361

POPCORN VENDING EMPORIUMS /
Attaboy Popcorn

Here's one business where opportunity really pops!

Popcorn is a great business to get into because not many products sold today offer the markup of popcorn. Your material cost for a $1 box comes to about one-fifth of your selling price—a paltry 20 cents. So get ready to make some money!

Selling popcorn is automatic once you have a good location. The sign and aroma of this age-old product acts as your beckoning salesperson. Any spot where lots of steady foot traffic flow will provide you with a nice, steady profit. Popcorn concessionaires, as they are called in the business, often prefer to move from spot to spot, following high-traffic gatherings such as sporting events, trade shows, and fairs. This is where you'll find *real* action! We found one happy popcorn vendor who specializes in high school and college football games, and others who make a small fortune at home shows, boat shows, and trade shows. Another successful operator works only concerts, fairs, charities, and auctions and confesses to earning as much as $1,000 every weekend.

Of course, there are popcorn wagons, popcorn stands, and popcorn vendors, but there is only one Attaboy concept for selling popcorn. Attaboy gives you a total and proven concept for making even *more* money in the popcorn business than even the most successful popcorn vendors consider possible. Under the Attaboy program, you attract throngs of popcorn customers with a distinctive and charming replica of an antique popcorn wagon which evokes the romance of a colorful bygone era. Each Attaboy wagon, decorated with authentic brass lamps, gleaming pull-up bars, brightly colored awnings, wooden wheels, and even an optional trailer, allows you to follow the crowds with a touch of nostalgia.

From your attractive Attaboy wagon, you not only vend delicious (and healthy) popcorn, but sell other complementary and equally profitable snack and beverage products as well. Attaboy furnishes you special decorative containers and all the other doodads you need to make your business a popping success.

Attaboy virtually ensures this success with a complete training program (no previous experience or special skills needed) to thoroughly acquaint you with the maintenance of your equipment and Attaboy's special methods for effectively merchandising popcorn. Attaboy also offers advertising assistance (the company would love to test some of your own marketing ideas) and, most importantly, assistance in finding those profitable, high-traffic locations. There are even a financial adviser and a legal staff to assist you should professional services be needed.

Attaboy's program in a nutshell is a low-cost way to get yourself into a high-profit business the right way. And best of all, there's no costly overhead. In many high-traffic areas, an Attaboy Popcorn Emporium ($13,000 to $28,000) can pay for itself in less than one year while you still take home a very good week's pay.

This is a turnkey business with no additional costs or future royalties or fees. You pocket *all* the profits!

This is a perfect part-time business to operate because there are so many opportunities to sell popcorn during evening hours and on weekends when leisure events take place. With your portable Attaboy wagon, you can work when you want and where you want. And it's an easy business to expand because you can finance additional Attaboy wagons from the profits of your existing wagon and staff your growing empire with employees who will work for relatively low wages.

In good times or bad, people always want popcorn and can afford popcorn. Popcorn is healthy and universally popular, and with Attaboy on your side, extremely profitable.

For more information, write to

Attaboy, Inc.
P.O. Box 812
Minocqua, WI   54548
(715) 356-4127
Contact: William Bennett

CHIMNEY SWEEP SERVICES / August West Systems

Chimneys need to be cleaned and maintained on a regular basis to prevent a dangerous buildup and combustion of creosote. Even the smallest accumulation of soot can be a threat to home safety, and there are millions of dirty chimneys out there just waiting for disaster to occur.

If you've ever witnessed a chimney fire, you've seen the volcano-like eruption with flaming balls of creosote spewing out the top of a chimney with the force of a jet engine. And you've heard that unmistakable roar that sounds like a locomotive charging into your living room.

If you haven't seen such a fireworks show yourself, ask your local firefighter for a description. It's a nasty sight, and he or she will tell you all about the thousands of chimney fires causing millions of dollars of destruction, thousands of injuries, and hundreds of deaths each year. There's really only one way to prevent these disasters from happening, and that's to clean a chimney before it catches fire. This is where *you* enter the picture—as a professional chimney sweep with August West Systems.

The *Mother Earth News* calls August West "the Height of Technology," and we must admit there's nothing else like it in the world. Simply stated, August West Systems provides you with everything you need to be your own boss in a chimney cleaning business of your own.

Included in the system is a high-powered, high-volume dust collection unit that utilizes state-of-the-art filter technology. August West calls this machine the SootSweeper, and it allows you to efficiently clean a chimney in record time and to guarantee cleanliness to your customers. That means no worries about white carpets. It also means a dollar-per-hour fee that just can't be beat.

19

Part-time or full-time, it all translates into the same thing: Dollars in Your Pockets! Lots of them—made more efficiently than you ever thought possible. But it's what you're doing that really counts—saving people's lives.

You can make more than $55 an hour in this business. This translates into earnings of nearly $1,000 just working weekends. No wonder they say chimney sweeps are cleaning up.

August West Systems is an industry leader and can really show you how to succeed in this easy-to-operate business.

For less than $2,000, August West provides you with everything you need to start making money immediately. That includes equipment, training, newsletters, workshops, advertising and promotion ideas, and even a top hat. Master Card and Visa are accepted, so you can pay in monthly installments if you wish.

There are thousands of homes right in your own community that need a chimney sweep right now. And they will need a chimney sweep again and again—about once every two to three years if they want to keep their chimney safe and clean. This means that you can quickly build a strong customer base and guaranteed repeat calls, because other chimney sweeps are indeed difficult to find.

Yes, you'll get your hands (and just about every other part of you) dirty, but what's a little dirt when you are making so much money as the beloved town chimney sweep complete with broom and smile?

For more information, write to

August West Systems
38 Austin Street
Worcester, MA   01601
(617) 753-5544
(800) 225-4016

IMPRINTED BADGES / Badge-A-Minit

Everyone has a favorite "message-flashing" button for his or her lapel. So if you want to make big money, there's no time to waste. With a Badge-A-Minit system you can make and sell popular pin-back buttons and make *very* good money in your spare time. These big, colorful 2 1/4" plastic-coated buttons are fast and fun to make and easy to sell.

Everyone loves message buttons. Contract with schools, churches, political candidates, service organizations, or booster clubs to supply their buttons. Buttons are also big sellers in stores and shops, or you can sell them at fairs, flea markets, or just about anywhere else people congregate.

Take any slogan, message, emblem, design, or even photo and you can put it on a button in less than a minute (in even less time with a Badge-A-Matic). You can design your own buttons, choose from over 1,500 colorful, popular preprinted designs, or have Badge-A-Minit's art and print department design a custom message. You can also put button designs on custom key chains, purse mirrors, jewelry, and even yoyos. Buttons can say anything and belong anywhere.

Whether you want to start out small or with a bang, Badge-A-Minit has a kit that's perfect for you. The starter kit is a great way to get started.

The Badge-A-Minit starter kit contains everything you need to capitalize on this fun and profitable button business. For only $29.95, the lowest price anywhere for a complete button-making system, you'll receive.

A steel reinforced Lexan hand press,
A set of precision molded, color-coded assembly
  rings,

Enough metal fronts, pin backs, and plastic
covers to make ten buttons,
Ten preprinted humorous artwork designs,
Easy-to-follow instructions,
A full-color idea book,
"Look What You Can Do with Badge-A-Minit."

The Bench System at $49.95 was created for larger quantity button-making with its easy tabletop design. Serious button-makers will want to consider the Badge-A-Matic. At $299.95, this semi-automatic machine allows you to make a button in 12 seconds. Or choose the Badge-A-Matic II at $795.95. This all-electronic system does all the assembly for you in just two seconds! The exclusive Trade-up Offer allows you to start out small and trade-up to a larger capacity machine as the need arises, and you will receive full credit for the original purchase price of your existing machine. The capability of your machinery can actually grow as your business does!

Learn to use Badge-A-Minit's button-making equipment in less than half an hour. Professional looking buttons can be made in less than one minute once you review the simple step-by-step instructions that come with each kit. Badge-A-Minit provides a toll-free number if you need help or assistance with any part of the process.

Since buttons can be made in any quantity, costs and selling price vary. However, profit potential can run as high as 300 percent on the sale of finished buttons. Consider that you can make as many as 250 buttons an hour with Badge-A-Minit's bigger machines, and you can see the earnings potential on large quantity orders.

This is an ideal spare-time opportunity. It is particularly recommended if you are selling to the same market, or have related products.

To help you get started, Badge-A-Minit includes a booklet inside every catalog which is full of ideas for button uses. Every owner of a Badge-A-Minit system also receives, twice yearly, a magazine full of articles about customers and their successes in the button business. The magazine also contains unique designs and uses, and 12 free ready-to-use designs, never seen before. Badge-A-Minit offers a FREE 44-page catalog and idea booklet. All Badge-A-Minit products carry a lifetime guarantee.

For more information, write to

Badge-A-Minit, Ltd.
Dept. BST89
348 North Thirtieth Road
Box 800
LaSalle, IL   61301
(800) 223-4103
In IL: (815) 224-2090

BARTER AND TRADE EXCHANGE / Barter Connections

If you're a salesperson at heart, confident in your negotiating skills, and fond of day-to-day challenges, you could join the ranks of "barter entrepreneurs," who earn as much as $300,000 a year. Even a small-scale, out-of-the-home operation can net a sharp organizer $50,000 before taxes.

Bartering goods or services without cash has all the ingredients of a glamour business in which you can literally make a fortune. But it requires clever promotion, good organization and sharp sales ability. Heavy selling to get new members into the club, and hustle to keep existing members happy and involved are the keys to success in this business.

But if you like meeting people, explaining ideas, keeping careful records, and enjoy good "business skills," you should do well in a business that has reached $15 billion in total market volume. "And the barter industry continues to grow at a steady pace," adds Ken Barron, president of the highly successful Boston-based Barter Connections.

Bartering systems such as Barter Connections replace currency with "trade dollars" or "credits," with each credit or trade dollar the equivalent of a dollar in cash. The bartering organization's client base—most typically business owners and professionals with goods and services in demand—is listed in a directory updated periodically and supplemented with weekly or biweekly listings. The directory and supplements are mailed to all clients, listing members' names, addresses, and phone numbers. Clients are grouped into appropriate business or service categories typically ranging from "Accountants" to "Zipper Repair."

Clients are issued either a checkbook or credit card similar to a Visa or MasterCard. In addition, an account—handled much like a commercial bank account—is opened in their name, with barter transactions monitored by the sponsoring barter service.

The barter exchange makes its money through one-time initiation fees and annual dues, along with trading fees, typically 10 percent of the amount transacted. Trading fees represent the bulk of barter-club income, with salespeople constantly working the client base, reminding members of the advantages of bartering and encouraging use of member products and services. Considering the enormous volume of products or services that can be bartered through a system, potential earnings are enormous.

Most barter transactions occur close to home, so potential clients are business owners and professionals who live in your immediate area. However, the key to a successful operation is attracting a client base of those with products or services in strong demand. Accountants, ad agencies, restaurant owners, attorneys, doctors, interior decorators, and dentists are examples of members who can promote active trading.

However, products and services in demand cover a wide selection ranging from manicurists to architects and even belly dancers. The possibilities are endless. Even nations barter. The Soviet Union extended rights to manufacture Stolichnaya vodka to Pepsi-Cola for the rights to make Pepsi. In another instance, a leading barterer recently pulled off a trade of bat manure, an excellent fertilizer, for imitation mayonnaise.

Very little front-end capital is needed to start this business, provided overheads are kept low, and you can substitute drive for dollars. You can start this business from a home office with only a desk and personal computer to track barter transactions.

To succeed, you will need plenty of savvy on how to quickly build a profitable membership base and a few tricks of the trade to generate maximum income. That's where Barter Connections can help you. As one of the nation's most successful barter exchanges, they can provide a complete turnkey program and training with costs that range from $7,500 to $15,000 depending on the locale, prior experience in similar businesses, and related factors.

There are no additional royalties and since this is not a franchise you operate under your own name.

This is one business easily started on a spare-time basis. As membership expands you can gradually develop it as a full-time venture, employing commission salespeople to pitch potential clients and create sales activity amongst existing members.

For more information, write to

Barter Connections
850 Boylston Street
Chestnut Hill, MA   02167
(617) 738-8800

ADVERTISING SPECIALTIES / BASCO
Business Advertising Specialties

Before we get into the nuts and bolts of how you can get your share of the $4 *billion* advertising specialties business, let's look closely at the industry and how it works.

A robust business, advertising specialties is divided into four basic categories: advertising specialties, business gifts, premiums and incentives, and printed souvenirs. BASCO's unique imprinting machine lets you expand into a new and exciting fifth category: contract imprinting. Your market is vast. Every business, every professional, every manufacturer, every organization is your prospect!

BASCO invites you to participate in this big-demand, high-profit contract imprinting business, and it is going to provide you with the tools that give you a big edge over the competition—a huge, varied source of advertising specialty products, amazingly low (below wholesale) prices, a low-cost printer that prints on almost any surface and shape, plus technical and business assistance to guide you to success. As a contract imprinter, you provide companies with a wide line of attractive promotional items that can bear the customer's imprint (name, logo, and so forth), and make a hefty profit on each item sold. Some companies order tens of thousands of promotionally imprinted products each year, so you can see the attractive income possibilities.

Why is BASCO such a great opportunity? In the first place,

BASCO enables you to participate in this lucrative business for a very modest fee. For the first time ever, a person can enter the advertising specialty field as a part-time or second-income business and reap the combined profits of a supplier, distributor, and imprinter.

Second, as a BASCO associate, you are provided with detailed instructions on how and where to sell all five classes of merchandise. Not only does BASCO tell you how to sell, but it backs up the information with effective letters to different types of business firms, as well as other high-powered materials and samples to win over potential customers.

Third, BASCO publishes a complete full-color catalog, illustrating and describing hundreds of items that are widely used for advertising specialties, premiums, business gifts, and souvenirs. You can offer your prospects a choice of items, or better yet, select several you think are most appropriate for their needs and take samples along when you call to sell your BASCO line.

Fourth, the prices of the merchandise you buy from BASCO are far, far less than those other advertising specialty representatives pay. Think what that means in extra profit—if you sell at the same prices, you probably will make twice the profit competitors can from the same sale. But, equally important, you have a big price advantage to beat the competition's prices hands down.

Finally, you have exclusively available to you the only professional, low-cost pad printer on the market. You not only make money on the imprinting (up to $75 an hour, or even more!), but you control delivery time and quality. This means you can do imprinting cheaper, more quickly, and better!

Yesterday the door to a $4 billion industry was closed to you. BASCO just opened it. Come on in! Until now, the advertising specialty business, long controlled by a few thousand suppliers and their associations, had all the action. It was almost impossible for a "small" operator like you to break into this lucrative business. No more!

You can make several hundred dollars a week in your spare time as a BASCO dealer. Work your own hours; you have no boss to answer to when you put yourself into this ever-growing advertising specialties business.

For more information, write to

BASCO
9351 DeSoto Avenue
Chatsworth, CA   91311
(818) 718-1506

PRESSURE WASHING /
Black Magic

You wouldn't mind expending a little elbow grease to make $300 or more a night, would you? We didn't think so.

Let us show you how to make $20,000 a year part-time, or $35,000 to $50,000 or more full-time, with your own professional pressure washing service. These figures are *not* estimates. They're actual examples of what ordinary men and women like you are making right now cleaning restaurant kitchen vent systems using Black Magic Pressure Washing equipment and training. In fact, it's so profitable, most people pay off their small initial investment and begin to show a clear profit in only their first few months of operation.

Consider that every restaurant near your home needs this important service. In most places it's required by law. Yet there's a definite shortage of people trained and equipped to do the job professionally. With Black Magic's specially developed equipment and proven techniques, you can power off dirt and grease from range hoods and kitchen ductwork faster and more efficiently than with any other method—and make substantial profits while you're at it! You'll be your own boss, set your own hours, and provide a much-needed health and safety service to boot!

Do it yourself or hire a crew. Black Magic shows you everything from how to use the equipment to how to successfully build and manage your business. Plus there are other ways to earn great money with your Pressure Washing system.

Why did we pick Black Magic as one of the *100 Best*? There are four good reasons: First, there is exceptionally high demand for this service (there are about 800,000 restaurants alone needing this service!), and virtually no competitors. Repeat business and contract work are the norm. Second, pressure washing is mostly nighttime work. You can start part-time and keep your present job. Third, you have a broad market. With Black Magic you can clean a number of items—swimming pools, boats, buildings, and much more—so you are never without waiting customers. Finally, with Black Magic you have the finest equipment and most-complete training available, including videos and optional seminars for "hands-on" training. The unique sales promotion kit helps you build a customer base fast. Best of all, this is not a franchise—you keep every single penny you make without paying costly franchise fees.

This is an easy business to learn. With Black Magic training, you can be an expert in this widely needed service in a matter of hours. Black Magic continues to work with you and to provide close dealer support to ensure a successful operation year after year. Your investment can be recouped in only a matter of months, or even less if you more actively seek accounts. Think of the money you can make—up to $1,000 just to wash a full-size swimming pool! And most Black Magic dealers say that if they had the time, they could triple the number of clients.

Yes, it may take a little elbow grease to operate your own Black Magic business, but we know of no other business where your efforts are so well rewarded.

For more information, write to

Black Magic
1489 Mountain Road
Stowe, VT   05672
(800) 334-3395

"SICK" BUILDING SERVICE / BriteTech International, Inc.

Rhubarb sauce generally evokes, at best, vapid reactions. But for Terrance Robson, president of BriteTech International, Inc., it inspired a new company. Perhaps a brand new industry.

The onetime Minneapolis wunderkind, who by age 35 had already launched two successful companies that would blossom into innovative franchise industries, has embarked on his most far-reaching—and most promising—endeavor yet: BriteTech International, Inc.

Based in Atlanta, BriteTech is a specialty service franchise committed to eradicating environmental ills contributing to what Robson colorfully calls "Sick" Building Syndrome (SBS), by restoring and protecting virtually any surface damaged or infected by pollutants, chemicals, stains, bacteria, or acid rain.

Robson's company analyzes interior environments from ceiling to floor to identify polluting contaminants. It then cleans and treats areas with specially formulated compounds, sealing and protecting all surfaces to retard further contamination. BriteTech also supplies maintenance crews with a wide array of products designed to ensure continued protection.

At the core of BriteTech's effective assault on these costly enemies of business, industry, and personnel are some 20 proprietary formulations developed by Robson and the company's resident chemist. All are nontoxic, biodegradable products that might not have been developed were it not for Grandmother Robson's rhubarb sauce.

It all started when Robson headed AcoustiBrite, an acoustical ceiling tile-cleaning company. "One of my clients was plagued by permanent rust stains on concrete, wood, even on employees' clothing," recalls Robson. "My initial research into rust removal was futile. Then I remembered how my grandmother used boiled rhubarb sauce to clean rust from her aluminum pots. It was a natural, organic cleaner." Robson analyzed the properties of rhubarb, determined that the plant's oxalic acid acted as a cleaning agent, and developed a product that literally made the rust stains disappear. With the assistance of chemist Cliff Cantrell, president of Atlanta's Salient Corp., Robson developed equally impressive and unique formulas to remove stains (such as blood, iodine, tar, dyes—virtually anything—from masonry, metal, wood, fabrics, and so forth), to prevent stains, to literally eat odors caused by molds and bacteria, to destroy indoor pollutants, and to protect outdoor structures from the ravages of acid rain. Robson is no rube when it comes to rhubarb.

Robson points out that when "new or unique problems are encountered, our R&D division is capable of custom-formulating solutions to meet the needs of clients."

Only six months after opening its doors, BriteTech International had sold 16 franchises. By the mid-1990s, Robson projects network-wide revenues of more than $20 million, from at least 45 operating units.

One reason for the company's ultra-fast franchise growth is the virtually untapped market of endusers—from international corporations and hotel and restaurant chains to local hospitals, retailers, manufacturers, and schools—not to overlook even governmental agencies. The franchise fee is $15,000-$25,000, with total start-up costs of less than $10,000 including working capital. Franchisees can be operational within 30 days, initially working from their homes.

"An important factor in our success has been the escalating concern about Sick Building Syndrome (SBS)," says Robson. "Environmental hazards in the workplace are costing employers billions of dollars in lost productivity and potentially billions more in pending and anticipated toxic tort law suits."

The Environmental Protection Agency estimates that as many as one in three buildings across the United States is "sick." The governmental agency's research reveals that levels of some indoor air pollutants "may exceed outdoor levels by 200–500 percent."

This is one opportunity that offers unbelievable growth potential, and it's a business that's easy to learn and to operate in your spare time.

For more information, write to

BriteTech International, Inc.
6350 McDonough Drive
Norcross, GA   30093
(404) 449-8244

ACOUSTICAL CEILING CLEANING / Ceiling Clean

When it comes to ceilings, one of mankind's better ideas was the acoustical ceiling. But that was before someone had to figure out how to clean those sound- (and dirt-) absorbing tile and textured ceilings. One firm successfully combating this problem is Ceiling Clean of Las Vegas, Nevada. President Richard F. Papaleo first became involved with this heads-up business in the 1970s. "We were in the janitorial service business and had customers with dirty acoustic ceilings and no way to clean them," he says, "so we started to investigate ways to attack the problem."

Today, Papaleo is keeping busy manufacturing acoustical-ceiling-cleaning equipment and chemicals, and has built a strong national demand for his products. Ceiling Clean has more than 300 full- and part-time operators in the United States, and 21 foreign operators from Hong Kong to England.

The ceiling-cleaning market is expanding fast. According to Ceiling Clean, 75 percent of the 20 billion square feet of acoustical ceiling tile the firm has installed since 1960 is still in service today. With the industry producing over 1 billion square feet of new acoustical ceiling annually, there appears to be no end to the cleaning business potential or its money-making possibilities.

Ceiling Clean helps its dealers find their own customers and also provides them with a very successful marketing program. For example, Ceiling Clean recently produced a very professional video sales presentation to help dealers more effectively sell this unique business so customers instantly buy their service. The firm also keeps careful track of how many of its dealers are located within a certain area. "We have a dealership program in which we assign people to a given area by population. However, they are not limited to that area. To help maximize our dealers' incomes we just control the number of our people in a specific region," Papaleo adds.

Although always interested in expanding, Ceiling Clean has been careful when adding new dealers. "First, we determine if there's a Ceiling Clean dealer already operating in the area," says Papaleo. "Then we determine which people can readily represent us. If the market area is available, we're usually willing to place an operator there." Once a new owner is set up in business, Ceiling Clean keeps in touch through a monthly newsletter. "We want constant communication," says Papaleo. The firm's long-term objective is to get enough operators to represent Ceiling Clean in virtually every corner of the United States.

Equipment includes two specially designed machines for product application, various accessories, promotional material, and an expandable supply of stock, which, if used properly, represents about $11,000 worth of sales. All new operators receive two days of factory training at the firm's Las Vegas headquarters, which includes transportation and lodging. Although used primarily for cleaning acoustical ceilings, the equipment can also be used to clean walls, vinyl wall covering, or other washable surfaces, which offers even more profit potential for ambitious dealers.

"We know," Papaleo says, "that the two major reasons for business failure are improper knowledge of the business you choose and lack of funds. We have tried to design this business to overcome both of these basic causes of failure and eliminate them as much as possible." Operating a Ceiling Clean business can be either a full- or part-time proposition, with many people working out of their homes.

There are very few buildings that exist that would not benefit from Ceiling Clean's unique and profitable service. Customers such as McDonald's, IBM, JC Penney, Sears, numerous hospitals, power companies, telephone companies, and every kind of business you can think of have enjoyed the benefits of using this cost-effective service.

The dealership program is not a franchise, so there are no franchise fees or ongoing royalties to pay. All that is required is the purchase of equipment, which includes operating supplies, promotional materials, and the training in Las Vegas. The total price of $9,800 includes round-trip air fare, and two nights' lodging.

There are very few highly profitable businesses available today with such a modest investment. Many entrepreneurs are discovering why this unique business is a proven winner—endless demand and no competition!

One Ceiling Clean dealer in Los Angeles did $3,000 worth of work in his first week. He's constantly booked solid with additional jobs. Another dealer, in Atlanta, grossed $4,950 one week after completing his factory training. Every day Ceiling Clean receives calls from dealers telling about their high-profit jobs in offices, factories, schools, homes—just about anywhere there are dirty ceilings!

Cleaning ceilings may not strike you as a glamorous business, but there are very few opportunities with such virtually untouched expansion possibilities. You can choose your own hours and gradually build a full-time business and one you can easily expand by training new employees.

The key to your success is simply showing people how bright and clean their ceilings can be with Ceiling Clean!

For more information, write to

**Ceiling Clean Division
D.P.L. Enterprises, Inc.
5115 S. Industrial Road, Suite 506
Las Vegas, NV   89118
(702) 736-4063**

PROFESSIONAL CEILING CLEANING /
Ceiling Doctor International

Bacteria buildup along with general dust and grime in a ceiling can be a major health hazard in any office, commercial building, or even residence. The need for a professional ceiling-cleaning service can be seen with an upward glance in almost any office, according to Kaaydah Schatten, founder and president of Ceiling Doctor International.

"It is a vast market and most office maintenance firms do not include ceiling cleaning in their services," says Schatten, explaining that removing grime, dirt, and tobacco smoke from ceilings calls for specialized equipment, chemicals, and techniques.

The Ceiling Doctor process includes applying an atomized mist of proprietary chemicals under a pressure of about 1,000 pounds per square inch. Conventional equipment, she says, uses a pressure of from 50 to 150 pounds per square inch.

The Ceiling Doctor chemicals dissolve grease layers and static electricity charges that hold the dirt particles to ceilings and walls. Under high pressure, the chemicals blast free dirt particles, which drift to the floor and are vacuumed away. Before cleaning begins, all floors and furnishings are protected by special coverings. Amazingly enough, only the dirt is removed, with absolutely no damage to the ceiling tiles.

Ceiling Doctor, now a franchise company, cleans all ceiling and wall materials, including acoustical tile, stucco, wood, brick, concrete, dry wall, and vinyl.

Schatten states that her company's service saves up to 85

percent over the cost of replacement, formerly the only solution to badly discolored ceiling and wall surfaces.

"The ceiling cleaning business has been around for about 20 years," says Schatten, whose Toronto-based company, founded in 1983, is presently Canada's largest firm in its field.

"We updated techniques, acquired the necessary high-pressure equipment, created special cleaning solvents and developed a professional image for what used to be an overlooked part of office maintenance," she says.

Franchising began in 1987, and as of late 1989 there were 18 franchises in Canada and three in the United States, with many more on the drawing board.

Projections call for establishing 20 more Ceiling Doctor franchises in America before the end of 1989 and 30 new U.S. units in 1990. Eventually there will be 150 U.S. franchises. "We're looking for franchisee quality, not quantity," explained Schatten, who says plans are also under way to develop franchises in Japan.

"Our minimum market size requires a population of at least 400,000—large enough to contain enough commercial and professional offices, plus restaurants, to make a Ceiling Doctor franchise profitable and capable of great growth," she says, adding that residential ceiling-cleaning services will also be offered within a few years.

Schatten says that franchisees, following an intensive instruction program and on-the-job training, literally can "start at the top."

"We provide our new franchisees with a prospect base of local branch offices operated by our national and international clients," says Schatten, who reports that her company's clientele comprises more than 80 firms, including AT&T, Caterpillar, Chrysler, IBM, Johnson & Johnson, Xerox, Texaco, Merrill Lynch, Allstate Insurance, American Express, Beatrice Foods, A&W, Sears, Radio Shack, and other familiar names of corporations, insurance companies, financial institutions, governmental agencies, and retail and service businesses.

The fee for a single Ceiling Doctor franchise is $16,500. Each franchisee pays a 6 percent royalty on gross income and a national advertising fund fee of 2 percent of gross revenue. Master franchises for large metropolitan areas are also available.

Because Ceiling Doctor's service is of such high quality, you are assured a steady stream of customers. Ceiling Doctor can be operated full- or part-time and is highly rewarding financially, with possible incomes in excess of $700 a day. Ceiling Doctor should also be strongly considered if you now offer good companion services.

For more information, write to

Ceiling Doctor International
2200 Lakeshore Boulevard., West
Suite 105
Toronto, Ontario   M8V 1A4
Canada
(416) 253-4900

PICTURES ON A PLATE / Ceramic Glazing

Now here's truly a brand new, untouched, potential multi-million dollar business—turning ordinary photographs into permanent, high-quality, personalized giftware!

Picturegraphics—as this exciting new technology from Ceramic Glazing, Inc. is called—is the highly profitable business of permanently bonding any type of photograph to fine English dinner plates, cups, plaques—a complete range of fine China giftware.

The market is untouched because Ceramic Glazing, Inc. (CGI) is the only company with the easy-to-use picturegraphics process. And customer demand is exceptionally strong because the concept of framing a favorite photograph on a beautiful ceramic or China plate background is both novel and attractive and therefore a welcome alternative to ho-hum picture frames. Yes, a snapshot of your loved one can adorn your coffee cup, you can dine from a plate with the loving gaze of your golden retriever peering back at you, or you may choose to portray your entire family on fine China poised on your living room mantel. People find these possibilities irresistible, and this means everyone is a prospective customer.

Locate your picturegraphics studio in shopping malls, in flea markets, in gift or department stores—or even operate from your home. Advertise your service locally or rely on referrals from local giftware merchants and photographers. Display a few sample picturegraphic drinking mugs at the photo or gift departments of local stores and you'll have more business than you can handle.

Profits are exceptionally high because the end product has a high perceived value, and you have virtually no competition to contend with. You can make $200 an hour in this business, with little or no overhead if you have a good location or a strong retail referral network.

Picturegraphics is not a franchise and does not require a costly, high-risk investment. The complete package—including equipment and training—is only $4,850. There are no royalties to pay. You need no prior training in either photography (the customer provides the picture) or ceramics (you buy ready-made ceramics at low prices from recommended suppliers).

Your function is primarily to bond the picture to the ceramics using CGI's bonding process. Picturegraphics dealers often charge $10 or more for each item. (It takes only several minutes to complete the bonding process.)

This business is particularly profitable operated weekends in busy shopping malls. You can offer an instant photo service (think of the added income) and capture the impulse buyers as parents come walking through with their children. Picturegraphics is also a top seller in high-tourist-count locations, when people are more relaxed and receptive to interesting conversation pieces.

For more information, write to

Ceramic Glazing, Inc.
233 Georgia Avenue
Providence, RI   02905
(407) 856-0404

RENEWAL AND REFINISHING SERVICE /
Color Specialties, Inc.

Look around you, no matter where you are—in a restaurant, a bus, an airplane, a boat, an automobile, a church, a bowling alley, a bank, a hospital, in a school—no matter where you are, you will see scores of everyday items made from plastic, vinyl, man-made fibers, and leather.

Look closer. Notice how many of these finishes have cigarette burns, cuts or tears, or unsightly stains, or are faded or discolored!

What can be done with these items to solve those common problems? Sure, they can be replaced with new items, or perhaps they can have the damaged part of the item replaced. But the cost in either case is substantial, often much more than the original cost of the item itself.

That is, up until now! Now CSI (Color Specialties, Inc.) color technicians can easily solve all of those problems—and at a cost way below replacement—and far below the cost of replacing the damaged parts. And colors can be restored so fabric once again looks like it did when it was brand new.

A virtually untapped market exists for CSI distributors. There's plenty of work in theaters, stadiums, rest homes, and everywhere you look. Your only limits are the number of hours in the day and days in the week. Trained personnel are available to help at all times, and recruiting and training help are also available.

Within any given geographic area you literally can perform services that can be billed out at thousands of dollars per day. One operator can easily earn $100 per hour or better. Payment is usually made right on the spot.

Unless you are color-blind, CSI can train you in every phase of the business. You will learn how to master repair techniques, how to match any color, how to apply the color to any surface, how to find customers, how to operate your business profitably, how to be a part of the business community, how to master your time, and how to work with any type of customer. CSI will provide you all of this and more in a complete training program.

To ensure your success, you will be working with what the industry calls a truly amazing chemical. This newly discovered chemical is a water-borne product, nonflammable and odorless, that dries in minutes—a welcome characteristic that allows the reconditioned item to be used immediately. Any color can be custom blended right on the spot. You can apply the process in below-zero weather and in hot desert climates. In fact, you can work in any weather. The total product capability is thoroughly explained in the training program.

This is an exceptionally high-profit, low-overhead business. Your profits are an outstanding 94 cents of every dollar, so it will be difficult to find a more profitable opportunity.

There are now more than 450 successful CSI distributors, each with a fully protected territory that guarantees him or her a competition-free market and maximum earnings. But don't delay in checking out this opportunity, because territories are going fast!

You can start part-time, but most distributors prefer full-time considering the endless demand for their services. Your total investment to become part of the CSI team is only $18,600, which can quickly be recouped from two or three profits.

For more information, write to

Color Specialties, Inc.
6405 Cedar Avenue
So. Richfield, MN   55423
(612) 861-1555
Contact: Harold Toupin

AUTO TOUCH-UP / Color Tech System 1000

As new car sales decline, auto dealers must concentrate more on used cars and must spend more on their reconditioning. So get in on what *Entrepreneur* magazine (October, 1987) chose as one of the hottest businesses for 1988—auto detailing and color touch-ups.

Until now, auto paint touch-up work could only be handled by the large commercial auto repainting services. These firms, however, are generally interested in complete paint jobs, and few bother with touch-up work. When they do, it's for an exorbitant charge. The net result? Car owners and dealers with minor nicks and scratches have no place to turn for fast and economical touch-ups to improve the appearance of their cars.

But that will soon change! Color Tech System 1000 is a portable automobile paint touch-up system that enables you to precisely match the paint finish on 99 percent of the automobiles on the road. This complete and self-contained auto touch-up system is perfect for starting your own full-time or part-time auto touch-up business. And, because of Color Tech's easy-to-use technology and full ongoing support, prior experience is unnecessary.

Color Tech is *the* system that can put you into the highly lucrative auto touch-up business overnight.

As part of the Color Tech System 1000 system, not only do you receive ongoing support, but there are no royalty or franchise fees to pay. Your only investment is $1,295 for the entire system of inventory and equipment.

How many cars in your neighborhood have unsightly paint chips and scratches? How many of their owners would gladly pay $25 to $100 for a fast, professional touch-up that could make their car look brand new? You can start a route exclusively

45

serving car dealers and auto body shops, as other Color Tech dealers do. You can also advertise directly to car owners and handle jobs at their home, or even perform the touch-up while your customer is at work. Color Tech dealers report that they receive 10–15 calls a week—with minimal advertising. Expect plenty of referral business from gas stations, muffler shops, car washes, and other auto care centers that would gladly promote your service for little or no referral work in exchange.

Color Tech is also an excellent line to consider if you are now in the auto care business. For example, it's ideal for auto detailers, small auto body shops, and larger car washes that do light detail work.

Part-time earnings of $500 or more a week are common in this business, so investigate Color Tech System 1000 and get your share of the money to be made with this wide-open opportunity.

For more information, write to

Color Tech System 1000
579 Interstate Boulevard
Sarasota, FL   34240
(813) 378-1193

HEARING AND BREATHALYZER TESTS / Communidyne, Inc.

The folks at Communidyne, Inc. of Northbrook, Illinois have been responsible for providing entrepreneurs with a wide variety of money-making opportunities over the years. Their latest offering is a computerized breath analyzer that automatically computes an individual's level of alcohol consumption.

The Communidyne Model 2000 Breath Alcohol Analyzer has been found to amuse and entertain restaurant and bar patrons while providing an important public service as the talking unit encourages those who have imbibed in too much alcohol to stay off the road. This is one product that was long overdue!

Entrepreneurs can get into business by placing the units for a start-up cost of only $5,600.

As expected, local Mothers Against Drunk Driving, police departments, civic organizations, and Students Against Drunk Driving groups are getting behind local bars to install the units, and their endorsement can only be great for business all around.

Breath Alcohol Analyzer is a natural for the restaurant and tavern market—in fact, anywhere alcoholic beverages are served. Operators of these establishments are concerned about their liability for drunk patrons and will quickly see the merit of any product that will discourage their patrons from driving while drunk—while making healthy profits for themselves and you at the same time.

Sales of the Breath Alcohol Analyzer are already brisk. The company anticipates strong sales, and these units have proven exceptionally profitable.

Communidyne has a second exciting new product, also a terrific sideline item: a talking coin-operated hearing test.

Sixty million Americans suffer hearing impairment. Forty million of them suffer and don't know it. That's why we think

Communidyne's hearing test machine can be a fabulous cash business year after year. And start-up costs are less than $6,000!

The hearing test machine is a fabulous money maker installed in shopping malls, medical clinics, drugstores—just about anywhere. Consider how popular blood pressure vending machines have become, and you'll have an idea of what the demand may be for this useful device.

If you are looking for unique vending machines that are easy to place, serve a public need, and can earn you a serious part-time income, then Communidyne may have the dynamic duo you are after.

You can earn sizable commissions installing these vending machines at high-traffic locations. This is not a franchise, so you pay Communidyne no royalty or franchise fee. And it doesn't take very long to service a route. Spend only 10–20 hours a week and you can be collecting mountains of coins from concerned folks who for the first time can quickly and inexpensively discover whether they are alcohol impaired or hearing impaired.

For more information, write to

Communidyne, Inc.
636 Anthony Trail
Northbrook, IL   60062
(800) 562-5200

HOME-BASED COMPUTER AND TELECOMMUNICATIONS SERVICES / Computer Business Services, Inc.

Now it's possible to cash in from your own computer-based business operated spare-time (or full-time) from your own home.

Computer Business Services, Inc. (CBS), a leader in computer technology, now offers a dynamic and proven turnkey business any individual or couple can easily operate, even if they have no computer skills or experience.

The key to CBS's success is that it features four services—each in high demand right in your own area.

Electronic voice mail helps cut down on telephone tag experienced by so many key executives today. With greater accuracy and less cost than a live answering service, you can provide an efficient and economical alternative to anyone who's ever returned to a stack of pink "While You Were Out" slips on his or her desk.

Electronic bulletin board or voice messaging allows repetitive information to be accessed by any number of callers without tying to a live operator. Realtors, churches, and many other groups are finding that a phone robot is more efficient, and they are willing to pay reasonable fees for the convenience.

Computer telebroadcasting enables your system to dial hundreds of homes and businesses each day with your client's specific recorded message and then collects the names and phone numbers of interested parties for the client's sales staff to follow up on.

Biweekly mortgages, CBS's fourth service, are the hottest new concept in real estate! By paying half of their regular monthly installment every two weeks, homeowners actually pay 13 monthly payments each year, thereby saving thousands of dollars in interest. A 30-year mortgage, for example, can be paid in full in 21 years! Under the CBS system, you can give an exact computerized amortization to your clients, showing their savings over each month of the balance of their loan. Of course, the built-in telebroadcasting function can find you dozens of interested homeowners to sell this service to each month. A complete Bi-Weekly Presentation is included on VHS cassette, along with a portable video player and color monitor to make individuals with little or no marketing experience feel comfortable explaining the program right in a homeowner's living room. After the sale, you assist with the banking arrangements to process the biweekly installments, charging fees of up to 1 percent of the savings for the homeowner.

Considering the range of services, your home-based computer service can be in demand by any business or household in the country.

CBS provides the software you need if you already own a computer or will provide a complete IBM-compatible CBS-286 hardware/software package to start you in business in any or all four areas.

To help you succeed, CBS furnishes you with a three-point training program:

- Home office training sessions
- Home office training sessions on VHS cassette, along with thorough manuals
- Telehelp Service—telephone consultations by technicians who can literally "walk operators through all the computer's functions over the telephone and even troubleshoot any possible component failures."

Earnings potential is widely variable based on the hours you can devote to this new business. Several full-time operators have earned $4,000 to $10,000 a month—and some earn even more!

The time necessary to operate one or all of these terrific sideline businesses depends solely on your wants, needs, and desires. This business works equally well part- or full-time.

With only a relatively modest investment of $1,000 to $10,000, you can enter the booming electronic communications/ information industry with four easily sold services that can turn your computer into a gold mine.

For more information, write to

Computer Business Services, Inc.
CBS Plaza
Sheridan, IN   46069
(800) 343-8014
Contact: George Douglass

SELECT DISCOUNT COUPON PROGRAM /
Coupon Power

More than 250,000 billion manufacturers' cents-off coupons were issued in 1988. From breakfast cereals to soft drinks, cookies to toothpaste, manufacturers are turning more and more to the cents-off coupons you find littered across the pages of your Sunday newspaper as a way to win new customers and generate sales for their products. So why is it that you can never seem to find coupons for the specific products you use? Perhaps that's why only 4 percent of these coupons are actually redeemed each year. Consumers can never seem to find the coupons they need and want. But those coupons that are *not* redeemed are worth *real* money and can put *real* money into your pocket once you become part of a unique system that efficiently and economically matches coupon with coupon user.

Stephen and Susan Samtur (two smart cookies who know how to spot an opportunity) first sponsored their now highly successful Select Discount Coupon Program back in 1981. Their highly successful program now offers its members up to 1,000 national brand manufacturers' cents-off coupons of choice, helping their members save millions of dollars each year at the supermarket checkout counter.

So how can you fit into this terrific money-making idea? As a Discount Coupon licensee, your job is to sell this needed concept and helpful service to prospective members within your territory. You earn a hefty percentage of each membership sold—and also earn a generous percentage of the value of each coupon provided to the members you sign. Coupon Power does most of the work. It processes and distributes all coupon orders and supplies its members with a barrage of magazines, books, booklets, and other shoppers' aids, which makes Coupon Power a terrific money saver for every smart shopper in search of bargains.

You can easily sell Coupon Power memberships in 100 different ways—through flyers and handbills, at home parties, at bazaars and flea markets, in stores (yes, it can be a great promotional idea for supermarkets to help push the idea), and even on radio and TV shows. The Samturs have already been featured on dozens of radio and TV talk shows, so millions of ready customers are already familiar with the concept and only await you to approach them for membership.

Some clerical skills and organization are required if you are to maximize your income in this exciting program. Since most of the work is performed by the Select Discount Coupon Program, there is no inventory requirement or prepurchase of any kind.

Coupon Power is a unique service, so it's absolutely competition-free. You have this huge market all to yourself! Best of all, you can set your own hours and earn an excellent income offering this tremendous service within your community even 10–15 hours a week.

If you believe, as we do, that people want to save money on everyday items they routinely buy, this can be the spare-time opportunity you're looking for.

For more information, write to

Select Discount Coupon Program
106 S. Central Avenue
Elmsford, NY   10523
(914) 592-1647

COMMERCIAL CLEANING SERVICE /
Coverall North America, Inc.

Commercial cleaning is a $20 billion-plus industry in the United States, with projected growth to $35 billion annually by the mid-1990s. More and more businesses require cleaning on a daily basis. Commercial buildings, industrial facilities, and medical facilities all need professional maintenance, regardless of economic conditions. As new fields of business open, many more commercial cleaning professionals will be needed.

Coverall North America, Inc., with regional offices throughout the country, has become the leading franchisor in the commercial cleaning industry. Their franchise fees range from $3,250 to $14,000. Each franchisee receives a *guaranteed* gross monthly income! This nationwide motivated work force has been the key to long-term customer satisfaction and low turnover.

Coverall offers a carefully planned program that allows each franchisee to enter the commercial building cleaning field with the most thorough training and preparation. No experience is needed, as the training program, with step-by-step instruction, effectively trains the franchisee to be a commercial cleaning specialist in the shortest possible period of time.

Coverall's "performance-proven" method of comprehensive training for its franchisees is a training program developed by experts in the commercial cleaning field. Ongoing support, which include updating on new developments in the commercial cleaning industry and the latest innovation in cleaning equipment, supplies, and techniques, keeps you well ahead of the competition.

Earnings potential depends on the individual franchisee. Many franchisees start with the lowest possible investment and gradually build their business step by step from part-time to a successful full-time venture. Management seminars are presented frequently, giving each franchisee the opportunity to meet other Coverall franchisees and thus to exchange ideas that can benefit everyone. Coverall also provides additional cleaning contracts and customers, making it easier for your business to grow. Moreover, they thoroughly train each franchisee to obtain profitable cleaning contracts on their own.

To become a Coverall franchisee, there is no need to quit your job immediately. You can start your Coverall business while still being employed. Most commercial cleaning work is scheduled between 5 P.M. and 9 P.M., Monday through Friday, so there will be little interference with a regularly scheduled job.

The number of hours you elect to work will, of course, vary with the size of your investment. Larger investments require more hours; for example, 10–12 hours a month for the smallest gross monthly package and 65–70 hours for the largest possible gross is recommended.

Coverall offers several packages, depending on the income level you want. Prices range from $4,800 to $14,000 depending on the program selected. A portion of the franchise cost can be financed by Coverall, requiring a small down payment.

Franchisees are not required to buy equipment, supplies, or chemicals from Coverall. They do, however, receive a complete equipment and supply package when they first become Coverall franchisees.

Coverall North America, Inc. was established in 1982; there are now over 1,200 Coverall franchisees successfully operating. Many franchisees started with low down payments, and have grown from a one-person operation (or part-time) into a fast-growing enterprise with teams of cleaning crews. You can earn $20,000–$50,000 as a part-time Coverall franchisee. Income averages about $50 an hour; however, you can earn considerably more if you concentrate on selling new accounts and hire employees to undertake the actual cleaning services.

The success of the Coverall system has been featured in

many national newspapers, magazines, and periodicals. One reason we rate it five-star is that you have a proven concept in a recession-proof industry. In these turbulent times, that spells winner!

For more information, write to

Coverall North America, Inc.
3111 Camino del Rio North, Suite 1001
San Diego, CA   92108
(619) 584-1911
(800) 537-3371

PERSONALIZED BOOKS / Create-A-Book

Wouldn't it be great to be a publisher of what may prove to be the best sellers in America today!

You can now enter the publishing field even if you never intend to write a book. Create-A-Book company of Milton, Florida produces and markets a selection of 11 personalized books for kids. And each title is a best-seller.

Why? Each story can feature *any* child as the main character in the book, along with friends, hometown, age, and even the name of the person giving this unique gift to the child. This is the irresistible ingredient of the personalized book.

Founded by John and Karen Hefty, Create-A-Book seeks distributors who set up their own personalized book-printing business at crafts fairs, malls, or anywhere else kids can be found. Each book is personalized via a computer system with laser printer that offers unprecedented quality. In a flash, you have a quality book to sell.

The start-up cost is $3,995 and the entrepreneur must also have an IBM-compatible computer to run the software provided by Create-A-Book.

Books are purchased from the company for $3.00 each and are resold in the personalized format for anywhere from $12.95 to $19.95, depending on your market. You charge whatever you think your market will bear.

The Create-A-Book system is easy to operate even if you're not a high-tech buff. The start-up package comes complete with a lengthy and detailed videotape that takes you through the operation in an easy-to-follow, step-by-step fashion. Rely on Create-A-Book for plenty of ongoing support.

Create-A-Books are popular gifts and learning tools because kids love to see their name in print as a central character in an enjoyable story. Although the books are designed primarily for children, the company has received requests from all over the world to create books for adults, community leaders, grandmothers, corporate executives, and even pets. Everyone loves to see his or her name in print, so the market is unlimited.

You can easily earn $500 or more on a busy Saturday at your local shopping mall. Create-A-Book even offers an attractive kiosk, so shopping center developers will welcome you as a valuable traffic builder and tenant.

Create-A-Book has been successful for too many years to be considered just another fad. As a dealer, you can be assured that the winning Create-A-Book concept can be creating healthy profits for you year after year. And those profits can be substantial. It's easy to churn out a dozen or more books per hour, and with an average profit of $10 a book, your earnings potential can easily exceed $100 an hour—after *all* expenses. You can also sell Create-A-Book in large quantities through schools and other groups because educators realize a personalized book will motivate a child to read quicker than anything else.

There are other personalized book companies, but there is only one Create-A-Book. This is the team to team up with!

For more information, write to

**Create-A-Book
310 S.E. Caroline Street
Milton, FL   32570
(904) 623-9833**

COMPUTERIZED PHOTOS /
Creative Amusement Services, Inc.

Have you ever walked through a shopping mall and noticed throngs of people waiting to have their picture printed by computer? Chances are, it was another of Creative Amusement Services, Inc.'s (CASI) computerized photo stands. More than 5,500 successful CASI dealers now rake in the cash from a market that just seems to grow and grow and grow.

People can't avoid the temptation to have their pictures taken. They particularly enjoy computerized prints because it creates a totally different image than they are used to seeing with conventional photography.

Computers, videos, and instant pictures are three of the "hottest" businesses of this decade. When you combine all three, you have a sure winner. That's just what CASI did to make it one of the most successful businesses today.

With the CASI system, you take someone's picture with a TV camera and instantly print it out with a computer. It's so push-button simple, a child can run it. But the profits aren't kid stuff. It's an all-cash business and the profits come in healthy gulps. And it's not a franchise. There are no royalties or fees. The CASI system is portable, ready-to-go, and sets up in less than 30 minutes. You can set up shop anytime, anywhere—in malls, department stores, flea markets, resorts, conventions, private parties, and on and on. Travel with it. The world is your territory. You'll do business wherever there are people.

Absolutely no technical or photographic skill is needed to run your own operation. CASI offers complete hands-on training at its office, and additional training through its comprehensive instruction manual and videotape will help make you a master at the trade.

What can you earn? CASI has part-time system owners who pocket a few hundred dollars a weekend. (Not bad for 6-8 hours at your local flea market.) Full-time system owners in amusement parks and high-volume shopping malls often gross over $300,000 annually. The flexibility in earning is enormous—limited only by the number of hours you choose to work.

CASI also offers complete flexibility in programs, so start-up costs range from $5,900 to $25,000. But again, why not start with the basic equipment and gradually upgrade and expand from earned profits? You can keep your present job until your CASI income exceeds your present salary (which, based on the experiences of many CASI operators, doesn't take very long!).

There are several computerized photo franchisors, but we give five stars only to CASI, because with 5,500 happy operators, it's the biggest. Started in 1977, CASI also has the experience to ensure your success in what can only be described as one profit-filled and fun-filled business.

For more information, write to

Creative Amusement Services, Inc.
156 Fifth Avenue, Suite 323
New York, NY   10010
(800) 457-2274
In NY State: (212) 645-4770
Contact: Kenneth A. Kendes

PERMANENT LANDSCAPE BORDERS / Creative Curb, Inc.

Here's a brand-new opportunity to revolutionize the landscape business.

Now you can produce beautiful, permanent concrete landscape edging for architects, developers, and property owners and earn $100 and more—in your spare-time hours.

Creative Curb, Inc. has created its own market with little competition. Creative Curb is needed by just about every residential and commercial building in America today because it adds the finishing touch to lawns with a neat border that enriches appearance, improves property value, and ends unsightly edging.

With Creative Curb by your side, you start your own cash business immediately because Creative Curb provides all the equipment, techniques, and material you need to enter the multi-billion-dollar landscape industry with this unique service.

The Creative Curb complete start-up package includes its patented Creative Curb machine, a 16-foot custom-designed trailer, a 7.5-cubic-foot mortar mixer, complete accessory tool package, two-day training course, sales call binder, and more than 25,000 pieces of sales literature. Your investment? $21,995. No royalties. No add-on fees.

This is one service that's easy to sell, because once Creative Curb is installed at one home, the entire neighborhood becomes your ready and anxious market.

Profits are exceptionally high; your material costs are only about 10 percent of your price. And earnings are unlimited since you can easily train people to install curbing while you profitably spend your time selling new jobs.

It's easy to operate the Creative Curb equipment. You pour concrete mix into the machine and it extrudes a neat concrete border as you walk. Creative Curb can make any size, shape, or color curb quickly and professionally. Creative Curb can be installed around driveways, landscaped islands, or flower beds. Homeowners will be delighted to install Creative Curb because it ends messy landscape edges and can make any home or building considerably more attractive in only a matter of several hours.

Because Creative Curb has such excellent profit potential, you can earn your investment back in a matter of months. Creative Curb continues to support you with a dynamic marketing program to boost sales. You can start your own Creative Curb business spare-time or full-time, but because demand for Creative Curb is so high, we suggest you plan on a minimum of 20 hours a week.

It's not often that so revolutionary and exciting a new product is introduced. But we think we have the seasoned eye to spot a winner, and Creative Curb can be the one opportunity to make you a winner.

Creative Curb doesn't take your interest in investing lightly, so a step-by-step process is outlined to qualify you for this exciting opportunity.

For more information, write to

Creative Curb, Inc.
3002 Dow Avenue
Tustin, CA   92680
(714) 730-0500
(800) 847-6290

SNACK AND CANDY VENDING / Croatan, Inc.

Vending sales rose 11 percent in 1987 as volume topped $21 billion! Does that say $21 *billion*? Yes, it does. If you ever wondered why you would ever want to be in the candy and snack vending business, then that statistic alone should snap you to attention.

Now a word about the leader in the vending industry—Croatan, Inc.

As a professional marketing consulting company specialized in vending, Croatan offers a variety of reasonably priced equipment and extensive marketing support services to help you develop your business plan and route strategy for tapping the vending business for top dollar. How does Croatan do this? First of all, it is *not* in the locating business; instead, it has developed a very unique and successful location service that greatly improves vending business programs and assures success by helping clients position the best-selling products in the best-selling locations.

A great deal of excitement has been created by Croatan's unique business opportunity—"Catch The Wave!" If you want to own or expand a business that is capable of producing excellent returns and long-term growth potential, then Croatan is your answer and vending is the business.

The Croatan Vendor Program is very simple. When you are ready to start your route, you order the machine package (Plan) that best fits your requirements. That is what you order and that is what they deliver. In only a few days, you are in your own vending business! The only variable is that the unit cost of each vending machine depends on the volume of machines you purchase from Croatan at any one time. As with almost everything else you buy, the more you buy the less you pay.

The philosophy behind the Vendor Financing Program is that Croatan helps you build your business. How? Croatan provides additional machines (over and above your initial order) under it's unique financing plan. You make a 50 percent down payment and Croatan finances the remaining balance *interest-free*. This balance is paid to Croatan in 12 equal monthly installments.

When those machines have been making money for you for 90 days (and if your payments are prompt), they ship you additional Vendor-financed machines if you so desire. No hassles, no surprises, no sales calls from Croatan!

Should you want to capitalize on the benefits of volume sales (and inventory purchases), Croatan offers several other combination product and machine plans. Several vending pros on the staff constantly research new ideas to discover "hot" products. Whether you want to expand or diversify your line, just give Croatan a call. In addition, once you are established as a Croatan vendor, certain financing alternatives become available to you that are not offered to vendor "start-ups." Croatan's "on-staff" experts in vending procedures will work closely with you to build for you the most profitable vending business possible.

The vending business is a natural for spare-time entrepreneurs, because you can set hours that conveniently fit your schedule. That's one reason vending is so popular a business. But to really make money in vending takes "know-how." That's where Croatan excels. It knows vending merchandising like no one else. Croatan can show you what sells, how to price your products, and how to get top dollar returns on every machine. It's that expertise that makes the difference between winners and losers in the vending business.

If you are thinking about vending as your spare-time opportunity, you'll be mighty glad you joined with the folks at Croatan.

For more information, write to

**Croatan, Inc.
8136 Old Keene Mill Road
Suite B-109
Springfield, VA   22152
(703) 866-1002**

TRAVEL CRUISES / Cruise of a Lifetime

The cruise market is the fastest-growing segment of the travel industry. The all-inclusive feature of a cruise eliminates many hassles associated with other vacations. One price pays for everything, including round-trip transportation, lodging, meals, and entertainment. The market for cruises is so strong that more than $2 billion will be spent on new and refurbished ships in the next five years alone.

As more ships enter the market, competition will increase and cruises will become even more affordable. Even now, the price of an average cruise has dispelled the notion that cruising is only for the affluent. According to one study conducted by an independent research firm, cruises demonstrate the highest degree of leisure-time satisfaction and interest levels of all vacation types for all demographic groups.

Cruising is still a young industry in its present form. Yet with the number of ships available, there is literally a cruise for everyone, regardless of taste or pocketbook. Still, only 6 to 8 percent of the traveling public has experienced the joy of a cruise, and that leaves an untapped market of 92 percent. Key industry leaders estimate that 40 million Americans should be cruising every year and would be if approached by knowledgeable travel representatives.

Now you can cash in on the lucrative cruise business without the hassle and overhead of operating your own full-service travel agency. Yes, you can own your own "Cruise of a Lifetime" agency, booking cruises for friends, relatives, and clients.

Cruise of a Lifetime is a home-based franchise business. Although anyone can enjoy and make money from this fun business, it is absolutely perfect for homemakers looking to prosper in their own spare-time business.

As a franchisee you earn 8 percent on all top-line cruise sales sold in your exclusive county—regardless of whether you referred the client or not. Four percent is paid in cash and 4 percent in cruise credits toward 100 percent free cruises for you to enjoy.

Cruise of a Lifetime gives you all the support you'll need. You receive an exclusive county territory, camcorder (to show all the great cruises available), fax, portable display, free weekend cruise, letterheads and supplies, and a full week of intensive training. Support is continuous. Sales experts are available to custom-tailor cruises to your clients' delight, thus making your job 100 percent promotional soft sell.

The total investment for this exciting franchise is only $8,250. But Cruise of a Lifetime extends 85 percent financing, so you can be part of the glamorous travel industry for only $1,250 down.

Exclusive territories are being sold rapidly, so we urge you to look into this wonderful spare-time opportunity without delay.

With cruises costing as little as $1,200 a couple up to $20,000 or more for an exotic 6–8-week voyage, the profit potential can reach many thousands of dollars each year. And don't forget, the travel business is basically a repeat business, so you can anticipate your clients coming to you for a different cruise each year.

For more information, write to

Cruise of a Lifetime Franchise Corp.
237 Park Avenue, 21st Floor
New York, NY   10017
(212) 551-3513

AUTO DETAILING /
Curtis Systems

Auto detailing is the ultimate in car cleaning and polishing. But don't confuse it with ordinary car washing—detailing is a skilled craft that makes cars LOOK and FEEL brand new again, using special chemical cleaners, professional equipment, and advanced polishing techniques.

People everywhere want their cars detailed. Car dealers and commercial auto fleets also use detailing services extensively. *Entrepreneur* magazine (October, 1987) described auto detailing as one of the "hottest" new businesses around. Even the respected Dun & Bradstreet estimates that gross sales for detailing could reach $2.5 billion by 1995.

Auto detailing is a great cash business. You can earn $100-$200 per car and up—for about 3 to 4 hours' work. You can make more than $1,000 a week averaging just two cars a day.

What makes auto detailing the Curtis way a true standout in a fast-growth industry is its total commitment to the success of the entrepreneurs now cashing in under the "Curtis System."

The Curtis System, which sells for about $2,500, includes a full set of equipment, complete training, and enough supplies to detail about 50 cars. After the first 50 cars, supply costs average about $5 per car.

"We're an information based company," say the Curtis people, explaining how important they feel training is. "You can have the best equipment in the world, but if you don't know the best way to use it, you're just not going to get the best results—and certainly not in the best time. That's why we put so much effort into our training video and manual."

Curtis' professionally produced 90-minute video uses sophisticated teaching techniques to demonstrate each step in auto detailing, including pressure washing, shampooing, vinyl cleaning, compounding, and polishing. Introductions and reviews to each of the detailing elements reflect the good overall organization of the material. Charts, demonstrations, close-ups, and freeze frames are just a few of the methods used to present the vast array of information.

The 190-page manual includes exclusive marketing information as well as details on how to write business plans, keep financial records, and care for detailing equipment. The manual expands on and reinforces information presented in the video.

"Initial training is just the start of the information we provide," claims Curtis. "We also have an excellent sales promotion package to help our customers turn profits quickly, and expert, free telephone consultation."

Important as training is, Curtis says the right equipment and cleaning compounds are essential to a successful operation. The Curtis twin-head orbital polisher is an important element of the system. It polishes all types of automotive paint and can also be used for shampooing interiors. Curtis maintains that it's the best in the business.

Good equipment and products are important, according to Curtis, but the most important ingredient in his formula for success is desire and willingness to work hard. "This is not a get rich scheme," he says. "But if you're willing to work hard to make very good money, detailing offers a great opportunity to own your own business without a big investment."

One great feature of the Curtis System is that it gives you a choice of programs so you can start with the system that is right for you. The *Professional System* gives you everything you need to work the fastest, easiest way possible. The Professional System is ideal for detail shops. The *Mobil System* is the way to go if you want to "set up shop" at your customers' homes. (Curtis even provides a portable tent, so you have a well-advertised shop you can set up in minutes.) The *Starter System* is just that—a way to start if you are simply looking to get your foot in the door at the lowest possible cost. But when you are as confident as we are about the Curtis System as a bona fide money machine, you will soon want to upgrade to the Professional System to maximize those dollars.

What makes Curtis truly unique as a car detailing company is the extent of its dealer support. Curtis not only offers the greatest flexibility in designing the detailing system best for you, but it backs it up with the support you need to become as successful as possible.

For more information, write to

The Curtis System for Advanced Automotive Care
Dept. 78, Box 250
Stowe, VT   05672
(800) 334-3395, Ext. 78
Attn: Carole Vasta

AUTO ACQUISITION CONSULTING / Davis Auto Network

In 1987, Vin Davis began his sixth year of employment with the automotive giant, General Motors. After being with GM's Labor Relations Office for more than five years continuously sharpening his negotiation skills, Vin began to reflect on the automotive industry and how cars were purchased. He noticed that automobile prices were constantly rising, whereas most consumer salaries were not—or at least were not rising quite as fast. Several months later, Vin started Davis Auto Network, locally known as DAN. DAN's objective is to provide auto buyers a much-needed service to save them the hassle of running from dealership to dealership, haggling with various salespeople at each agency to achieve a better purchase price. Vin believes his negotiation abilities and knowledge of the car industry give him a wide advantage over the average consumer, and therefore he can save them time, money, and the hassle of shopping. Vin also believes that in any negotiation, whether it be over a car, a house, disagreement, or whatever, the outcome should result in a win–win situation—in DAN's case, a win–win–win situation. Consumers win because they buy a car at a good purchase price, saving thousands of dollars; dealers win because they still make a profit and have a pleased customer; and DAN wins because it has a satisfied client and received a commission for its efforts. Vin perceives DAN's service to be the wave of the future. He also perceives the service to be valuable in both good and bad times. In good economic times, so many vehicles will be sold throughout the country that a good percentage of the buying market will utilize a service such as DAN's. In bad times, consumers will still have the need for auto transportation, but they will more aggressively seek the best price possible because each

70

dollar spent during recessionary times must be maximized. And what better way to maximize your auto-buying dollars than to have a professional buying service locate you the best car price in the area, unless you have the knowledge to do it yourself?

Because Vin has become so successful with his auto acquisition consultant business, he soon realized its potential nationwide and now trains others to be auto consultants right in their own areas.

For only $20 you can receive a Consultant Report that will open your eyes to the vast income opportunities within the auto industry. An investment of only $395 will provide you with the tools you'll need to start your own profitable service, as Vin has done.

This can be the perfect sideline business, offering exceptionally high income per hour. And it's a unique market, easily reached through target advertising.

To succeed in this business you must be willing to learn the auto industry and really know how to comparison-shop for cars. But here's a secret. As a professional consultant, car dealers know you are in a position to move so many cars every year, they'll automatically give you the very best price possible, and sometimes you can even buy at fleet rates, saving your client an additional $1,000 or even more. Average commissions are about $250, so if you shop for just one car a day, you can earn about $75,000 a year.

For more information, write to

Davis Auto Network
Box 26153
Trotwood, OH   45426
(513) 837-1171

LANDSCAPE AND CHRISTMAS LIGHTING
Dekra-Lite

One brand-new opportunity to catch our roving eye was Dekra-Lite, a franchise program that puts you into a niche business: installing landscape and Christmas lighting.

This business makes perfect sense to us because tens of thousands of homeowners want their home bathed in attractive outdoor lighting but either do not know how to effectively design lighting or do not want to incur the expense of hiring electricians to install such lighting.

Dekra-Lite's regular landscape lighting service features low-voltage lighting that can make any home a showcase at nightfall. Dekra-Lite has available a wide assortment of lighting fixtures to literally put each home in the best light. Start-up costs are only $500 (no inventory is required), so anyone can afford to take advantage of this opportunity. Demand for this service is strong; Dekra-Lite costs are extremely low, so virtually every home-owner is a prospective client. This unique service can also be offered to owners of small commercial buildings, resorts, golf courses, municipal parks—just about anywhere there is need for attractive, functional, and economical exterior lighting.

Although Dekra-Lite's regular landscape lighting program can provide a comfortable weekly income—even on a part-time basis—the real profit bonanza comes at Christmas. With Dekra-Lite you can also design, install, and remove decorative Christmas lighting professionally and economically. Installing Christmas lights can be a hassle for the average homeowner, yet most people enjoy a well-decorated home during the Christmas season. You can earn as much as $700 on a colorful Christmas installation (appreciably more with larger homes or for more elaborate installations), and most of this is profit. Once customers see how attractive their homes can become with the Dekra-Lite Christmas decorating service, you'll have their repeat business year after year. The Christmas lighting program requires $18,000 in start-up cost, but this is still a great investment once you consider the great profit potential.

No technical background or licensing as an electrician is necessary to join Dekra-Lite. The company provides everything you need to be successful and profitable. This includes equipment, access to a wide assortment of inventory and supplies, full training, and a comprehensive marketing program.

Dekra-Lite lighting services can easily be marketed through direct solicitation (you can see at a glance who can benefit from improved lighting in your neighborhood) or through local newspaper ads. A "before" and "after" picture can be worth a thousand words. There is continuing income from maintenance, and customers are always looking to upgrade their lighting once they see how much impact even basic lighting can have on the appearance of their home. Christmas lighting sells primarily through word of mouth as Dekra-Lite customers invariably have the most talked about home at yuletide season.

The two programs—the landscape lighting and Christmas lighting programs—are both available for one low franchise fee of $8,500. If you are in the market for a business guaranteed to turn you on, check this one out!

For more information, write to

Dekra-Lite
17945 Sky Park Circle
Irvine, CA   92714
(800) 888-8319

STUNT PLANES / Dipco Products, Inc.

Now here's an absolute "no-brainer" of a sideline business you can have a ball with and make nothing but money with too! All you have to do is sell "Dip-er-do," the patented "magic-in-the-air" airplane guaranteed to fascinate whether you are 7 or 70.

Probably one of the world's greatest impulse items, the Dip-er-do is the "original" precision indoor stunt plane that always comes back. Made in the United States, it comes completely assembled and ready to fly. There are, of course, other planes that boomerang back to you when thrown, but none are as well-made or designed with the high-performance precision and predictability as is the Dip-er-do. So aeronautically perfect, the Dip-er-do is now being used to show principles of flight in NASA's outreach program which teaches aeronautics and space-related topics to fledgling aviators and astronauts.

This is the very same Dip-er-do featured in a full-length story in "PM Magazine" in 1984. It was also seen on "60 Minutes," highlighting a story on an inventors' convention. This gem was even featured on "Good Morning America" during a Christmas "Perfect Stocking Stuffer" segment. Stories on the Dip-er-do have been done by the *Chicago Tribune*'s Bob Greene (syndicated in over 100 papers), the *Philadelphia Inquirer*, and New Jersey's *Business Magazine*. Because Dip-er-do is a very small family business with sales coming through dealer demonstration only, the potential sales surface has only barely been scratched. More than 30 million stunt planes have been sold, yet few airplane buffs have seen the original, authentic Dip-er-do— the one that always comes back. Yes, this is the same Dip-er-do sold at the Texas State Fair, the Intrepid Air Space Sea Museum, South Street Seaport, and hundreds of other locations where it dazzles the crowds every time.

Inventor Mike Stone now offers *you* the once-in-lifetime

opportunity to earn a small (not so small when you think about it) fortune selling the original Dip-er-do.

The market is huge. Since 1977, the Dip-er-do has been successfully sold at airport gift shops, museums, fairs, department stores, malls, toy stores, fund raisers, rock concerts—anywhere there is a high flow of people traffic.

Anyone can fly the planes (paper or styrofoam) with a little practice. Even if you're totally uncoordinated, you'll have little trouble. Certainly the gift of gab will help close a sale, but considering the Dip-er-do mostly sells itself, you don't have to say much to convince the crowds that this is the fun-packed novelty they have been looking for. If you're comfortable with people, you can sell a ton in any good location. Complete video-tape training almost ensures your success.

Dip-er-do is an indoor item. "Welcome to the World of Indoor Aviation." It is an ultra-light (weighs less than an ounce), high-performance glider that fascinates people by its patent predictability and precision engineering. It makes everybody smile.

The styrofoam Dip-er-do II has a lifetime guarantee. "You break it, they replace it" (for postage and handling costs). This crowd pleaser is virtually indestructible.

Once you buy the initial kit ($29.95 for $36.00 worth of retail product), the 400–500 percent markup on all additional purchases, no matter what the volume (minimums are nominal) are yours. No discounting is necessary because the product sells itself. All dealers buy directly from the manufacturer.

Part-timers selling Dip-er-do only one or two days a week pull in annual incomes of $20,000–$30,000. Work full-time (or sell from multiple locations) and watch your income skyrocket to six figures.

What does it take to cash in on what may be the next pet rock or hula-hoop? All you need is a small table, an easel with a sign, a smile, and a few Dip-er-dos—and you're in one great business!

For more information, write to

**Future Thunder Productions
245 East 63rd Street, Suite 612
New York, NY   10021
(212) 644-1637**

REMOVABLE-TATTOO PARLORS / Don Ling's Removable Tattoos

Welcome to the wonderful world of removable tattoos, and what is proving to be a real phenomenon in the amusement business.

Removable-Tattoo Parlors are popping up all around the country, due in large part to Don Ling's Removable Tattoos.

Don Ling's Removable Tattoos are a real money maker and crowd pleaser wherever you set up shop. The tattoos sell like crazy! They just seem to magnetically draw people to them. The reason is, *they're catching*! You don a tattoo or two in your booth, so customers see how great they look, and they're hooked. Once their friends see these great tattoos, they come flocking. Soon you have a long line of people anxiously waiting to spend $2–$25 or more for the fun of displaying one or more of Ling's great-looking tattoos.

You can easily make good money with this idea at flea markets, street festivals, fairs, resort areas, beaches, malls, or anywhere you find people—even if you don't have the advantage of working in an established fun park or traveling with a carnival. If Don can make more than $1,750 at a local street festival on a weekend while testing his crazy concept of removable tattoos, just think what you could earn in a resort area near a beach, working a good-sized flea market on a regular basis, or hitting the fair circuit! The possibilities are limitless, especially when you consider that you easily earn from six to ten times your investment each and every time you reorder!

Why are Don Ling's tattoos such great sellers? First of all, these tattoos are not painted on like some others. That competitive process is very time-consuming and requires a certain amount of artistic skill. In contrast, these washable tattoos are applied quickly and easily with no artistic skill necessary.

76

Don Ling's Removable Tattoos are predesigned by traditional Japanese and American tattooists, and then layered on an ultra-thin poly film which is then applied to the skin with water in only 10–20 seconds. After removing the paper backing (and waiting a minute while the tattoo sets), the tattooed area is washed, patted dry, and powdered with talcum powder, and excess powder is removed with a damp sponge.

The entire tattooing process takes less than two minutes, and the finished product looks as good as or better than a real tattoo! Endurable, they last for two to four days, don't wash off in the shower or while swimming, and can easily be removed when desired with baby oil. There are more than 200 beautiful designs to choose from, and since they do require a one-minute setting time, you can efficiently work on two or more people at one time.

Removable tattoos sell best in warm weather (they sell great all year long in warm climates) where people are constantly in shirt sleeves or swimming suits.

An *impulse* item, Ling's tattoos can really create a buying frenzy when the weather is hot and there are lots of people around, such as at fairs. Once you apply a few tattoos and prospects see how great they look, the rush is on!

People are attracted to Ling's tattoos for a variety of reasons.

Young men think they look "macho," women like the beautiful butterflies and roses, and older people think it's daring or youthful to display one. For each you fulfill a special fantasy, and why not spend a few dollars on a fantasy?

Since adults, teenagers, and youngsters all have that certain fantasy enhanced with a temporary tattoo, they actually do line up 20 deep to spend from $2 to $25. And with the increased popularity of tattoos among rock stars and film stars, there is new acceptance for the tattoo. Because there is no lifetime commitment with a removable tattoo, its popularity has increased even more.

Since the tattoos are applied so easily, no real skill is needed to succeed in this business. However, to successfully operate any business where you work directly with the public, a pleasant, outgoing personality is helpful.

Don Ling provides a brochure that goes into complete detail on the way to apply the tattoos, sell to customers, collect monies, and even land high-traffic locations.

The earning potential depends on the location, customer concentration, and, of course, the weather. But there is real money to be made! Some tattooists take in nearly $3,000 on a weekend at local street festivals; others say they earn more on a weekend with this fun business than they do the rest of the week at their regular job. A $300 package contains more than $2,200 in retail value, so you see how high profits can be!

The amount of time devoted, and therefore the earning potential, is up to the individual dealer. If you are working a fair, festival, or mall, you can make money every hour that they are open. If you set up on the beach, for example, stay as long as there is a lot of foot traffic.

As crazy as the idea sounds, more than 4,500 Don Ling Tattoo Parlors are now cashing in. What will it cost you to get in on this fun-filled business? Only $50 for your initial inventory of Ling's exquisite tattoos for what might be the investment of a lifetime.

For more information, write to

Don Ling's Removable Tattoos and Fantoos
Box 309
Butterfield, MN   56120
(507) 956-2024
Contact: Donald R. Ling

MINI-DONUTS / The Donut Man

Statistics show that donuts remain the most popular snack item in America today. The trouble is, it's difficult to find good donuts except at permanent roadside stands such as you find with Dunkin' Donuts or Mr. Donut.

But now you can operate your very own spare-time donut shop to go where the people are—at parks, flea markets, auctions, country fairs, sporting events, bazaars—anywhere there's a crowd. And the donuts you sell will be delicious.

Make more than $600 in just one weekend! With The Donut Man you have the most popular spot around. The mini-donuts practically sell themselves. Simply start your donut machine and get ready—the aroma draws a crowd of hungry customers straight to your booth!

It's easy to operate your own Donut Man Machine. People of all ages, trades, and backgrounds have been successful with the Donut Man business. No need to be a great baker or mechanic— the Donut Machine assembles in minutes, is completely automatic, and is amazingly easy to operate.

With the Donut Man equipment, you can churn out dozens of donuts each and every hour. Your little portable stand can satisfy the insatiable demand for donuts from even the largest crowds, and this is what makes Donut Man so profitable a sideline venture—the combination of exceptionally high hourly sales; low, low overhead; and even lower product costs.

Donut Man provides full training complete with manuals and ongoing support programs.

Best of all, with Donut Man you have your choice of a number of vendor programs. You can choose a small portable stand or pick the Donut Express Trailer that has everything you need for a truly mobile mini-donut business. Simply hitch it to your car on a weekend—head for the crowds, and return with pockets full of money.

A mini-donut stand is a fairly simple operation to run since the stand offers only one main menu item. All the successful operators we spoke to agreed that location, sometimes even more than the tasty donut, is a key to success. A mini-donut stand can be successful as long as there is sufficient foot traffic. This is one reason we selected the Donut Man opportunity over other franchises. Its trailer concept (The Donut Express) keeps you in the middle of the action wherever it may be.

This is a fun and exciting business to run. Once you see how much money you can earn with mini-donuts and the Donut Man product, you'll understand why we selected it as one of our *100 Best*!

For more information, write to

The Donut Man
9851 Thirteenth Avenue North
Minneapolis, MN   55441
(800) 328-8213

HOME AND BUILDING DEALER / Eagle's Nest Homes

Bob Breedlove has a low-key selling style. He found a program and a product that met his needs when he became an Eagle's Nest Homes dealer-distributor. The Eagle's Nest company provides distinctive modular homes that can be built quickly and economically, meeting a growing need and serving an ever-increasing market for low-cost, high-quality modular homes and commercial buildings.

Now the head of Etowah Building Systems, he says: "The decision was easy. The look of an Eagle's Nest home is distinctive. It is easy to erect. And the manufacturing facilities are outstanding." In short, Eagle's Nest produces winners!

Eagle's Nest homes, which are round, rustic, and capped with pagoda roofs, are also dramatic. Breedlove found that there are many advantages to round houses. They require far less space to build. Anywhere you can pour a foundation, you can build a modular unit. They are also adaptable to any terrain, whether mountainside or flat.

As an Eagle's Nest Homes representative you too can offer a proud line of factory-built home packages that are easily and rapidly completed for commercial or residential use. The independent representative relationship with the company permits flexibility of hours, varying degrees of marketing or construction involvement, and proven pricing and advertising methods. Eagle's Nest homes may be sold in various states of completion based on buyer needs and the representative's involvement in construction of the home.

There are no shortages of reasons why Eagle's Nest homes are consistently strong sellers.

All materials used in the construction of each Eagle's Nest home are of the highest quality, and thus assure a lifetime of comfortable living with a minimum of maintenance requirements. Construction is made to exacting specifications utilizing quality craftsmanship and high-tech design inside and out. Eagle's motto is, "No other custom designed home offers so much for so little."

The unique pedestal construction of the Eagle's Nest home eliminates the need for load-bearing walls, so interior design is open and spacious both around and above you. The upper level is cantilevered above the lower level, and beyond that is the airiness of a cathedral ceiling. The Eagle's Nest home allows for complete freedom of movement, freedom of design, and freedom to live unencumbered by typical "box-like" rooms. Summertime or wintertime—the living is easy!

Selling Eagle's Nest homes is ideal for people with access to prospective home builders. If you have building skills, you can make even more money participating with Eagle's Nest Homes in the construction of the home, but construction experience is not necessary to become an Eagle's Nest rep.

Eagle's Nest Homes provides extensive on-site construction training (so you can see how easily Eagle's Nest Homes come together) and also provides full marketing support through an independent marketing organization.

As an Eagle's Nest Homes representative, you can earn between $2,000 and $12,000 per package sold based on the manufacturer's retail price. However, you set your own retail price and thus control your own profit margins, which may be much higher.

There are no restrictions or geographic limitations on where homes can be erected. Representatives may market homes anywhere in the United States; however, territorial assignments are based on general areas of intended market concentration.

This is one business you can make serious money in simply by enjoying your own Eagle's Nest home as a model that will virtually sell itself to those who see it. Not only can you live in a great house (at very low dealer cost), but you can possibly earn enough in the bargain to fully pay for it.

For more information, write to
Eagle's Nest Homes
Route 5, Highway 20 East
Canton, GA   30114
(404) 479-9700

STUDENT SERVICES / Education Funding and Planning, Inc.

Education Funding (EF) is the only full-spectrum educational services company in the nation. Once provided strictly by EF associates, EF's many education-related products and services are now being offered through an exciting and financially rewarding independent licensee program. EF licensees are more than just an information service; they are an actual provider of money for college expenses via the EF financial services program.

EF licensees earn high profits —up to 400 percent per sale! EF licensees are full-service educational consultants, assisting families in college financing, career planning, college selection, scholarship matching, SAT and ACT test improvement programs, and general study skills improvement programs. In addition, new products and services are constantly under development by EF, assuring you even greater future profits. Due to their many services, EF licensees are not limited to marketing only to high school seniors. Students of all ages need the services offered by EF licensees, assuring you a broad market.

EF has a remarkable and highly effective "funding and services delivery system." Licensees are *not* responsible for providing any funding or actually processing any of the services. All of the services are provided and processed through EF's National Service Center. Services are, however, personalized in the licensee's name; therefore, each licensee has a direct relationship with his or her clients. Licensees simply sell their services; they accept from the student the total fees (set by the licensee) and properly completed application. They deposit the fees into their account and then pass along the completed application and a small processing fee to the National Service Center. The National Service Center processes the application and delivers the requested service to the clients. EF licensees can expect many years of repeat business and many referrals!

EF provides licensees with an A to Z training, marketing, and continuing education program. Because EF processes the actual services, no prior experience in counseling or educational services is necessary. Licensees need a willingness to succeed, must possess empathy, and should have a desire to help others. Each licensee's income is in direct relation to his or her efforts, which means each licensee is in complete control of his or her financial future!

Licensees can expect to earn high profits because the processing fees are so inexpensive in relation to the total fee paid by their clients. Yet the total client fees are very affordable (based on suggested retail), so almost everyone can afford the various services. Add to this the fact that EF licensees actually provide thousands of dollars in funding, many times more than their fees, and it's not unrealistic for licensees to earn in excess of $50,000 a year. Depending on a licensee's efforts and abilities, a six-figure income is more than possible. Each day the opportunity multiplies as demand for EF services continues to grow.

Because licensees are in business for themselves, they determine how many hours they wish to work. Part-time involvement is easy. Since licensees do not actually perform the various services offered, their time is spent only in marketing. Most of the marketing methods require little time to maximize returns. Licensees can spend as little as 10 hours a week and receive a strong financial return. And it is easy to reach the student market, so you can easily sell EF's many programs. EF provides sample ad slicks and other advertising aids easily placed in student publications. EF representatives can see as many as 30-40 students a week so they have a steady stream of applications to process—and money to make!

For more information, write to

Education Funding and Planning, Inc.
Licensee Dept.
P.O. Box 771888
Houston, TX   77215
(713) 771-0697

CORPORATE ETIQUETTE COUNSELING /
Etiquette International

For Judi Kaufman, president of Etiquette International, a division of Judi Kaufman & Associates in Beverly Hills, California, elite establishments are her office. At fine restaurants or country clubs, she often lunches with top corporate executives, instructing them in the fine points of proper etiquette. Seem like the perfect career? "Today, manners means more than just the right fork," states Kaufman, whose tailored training ranges from making introductions and circulating successfully in social gatherings to charity fund raising and handling international differences in manners. "Companies are constantly worried about getting their money's worth for business entertaining, yet important choices like lunch or dinner, or sit-down or buffet are being made randomly, and often in error."

Such diverse companies as American Cyanimid, First Interstate Bank, and Southern California Gas Company are among Etiquette International's client roster. Before she begins her training of corporate executives, Kaufman assesses each client's needs and problems by talking to colleagues and family members, including executives' spouses. She also obtains the clients' anticipated goals and often looks at their calendars in order to help them prepare for upcoming events.

Dubbed by one participant as "gourmet therapy," Kaufman's "Good Taste Is Good Business" seminars received nationwide coverage in such publications as the *Los Angeles Times*, the *Chicago Tribune*, and *USA Today*. Kaufman is also a frequent radio and television guest.

Kaufman's initial investment of $5,000 now brings her annual earnings in excess of $55,000. Currently, she is offering an

Executive Etiquette Start-Up Package for those who want to associate with her company, one of a handful in the country that specialize in this type of work. She stresses, though, "What I am offering is not a franchise, but rather an assembly of information designed to help a person get the content of this business going so that individuals can offer quality, uniform one-to-one and group programs."

The cost of the Executive Etiquette package is $1,875, which includes shipping and handling. "I'm sure you'll agree that this fee is substantially below what one would have to pay various consultants in public relations, advertising, and business in order to obtain these specific directions," assures Kaufman.

Included in the start-up package are the Executive Etiquette Trainer's Manual, Guidebook for Clients, and a Checklist, plus sample press release, query letter, ad, inquiry sheet, program confirmation letter, and proposal for corporations. Other items included are the Executive Etiquette client assessment form and recommended fees and schedules for individuals and corporate training programs.

If after receiving the start-up kit you desire further information, an optional one-day private training session is available for an additional $800. This option helps associates learn all the intricacies of training clients, including seating guests, making toasts, handling table manners, using conversational openers, and giving tips graciously.

Judi Kaufman has made money in her business because she realized that there is an unmet need to train people how to observe business-entertaining etiquette. This is one dimension of business commonly overlooked, but that the business community is rapidly responding to. Concludes Kaufman, "Anyone who entertains for business with the impression that the goal is strictly to entertain and satiate hunger is not only a poor host but an ineffective businessperson. When you're entertaining for business, you're talking about a bottom-line return for your efforts. Unless you can measure that return after each event, then you were unsuccessful."

This can be an ideal spare-time opportunity, and one of great interest to you if you are tactful, enjoy working with people, appreciate the need for proper etiquette as a business tool—and believe you can match Judi's success in marketing this service to local companies.

For more information, write to

Etiquette International, Div.
Judi Kaufman & Co.
Beverly Hills, CA   90210
(213) 858-7787

TAX PREPARATION /
Federated Tax Service

In 1988, 30 million people paid more than $600 million for tax return help! And you don't have to be a bookkeeper or an accountant to share in the growing tax-preparation field.

Imagine being in business with a partner who provides you with as many prospects as you can handle every year, year after year. Learn how to prepare income tax returns, and the partner (Uncle Sam's IRS) is yours! Of the 92 million people who file income tax returns every year, 30 million seek professional assistance. And, according to the largest tax-preparation company in America, they pay on average nearly $25 for the service. Once you know how to do it, the average tax return will take less than one hour to complete! How many tax returns can a trained preparer do in a week? Full-time, spare-time, on weekends, in evenings? You can figure for yourself the dollars trained tax preparers can earn.

The answer to this question may be the best news of all. Can you do simple arithmetic? Can you read and understand plain English? If you can answer "Yes" to both questions, you may be ready to embark on a most remarkable and rewarding spare-time or full-time career in income tax preparation.

Federated Tax Service's (FTS) training was designed to teach professional tax preparation to ordinary men and women, folks without special education or experience. Age, sex, or where you live is no barrier in the tax-preparation business. FTS has trained thousands of men and women from all walks of life, ranging in age from 17 to 70, and whether they live in big cities or small towns. Everything is spelled out in simple-to-follow words you use every day. Federated Tax Service will lead you step by step through everything you have to know to prepare tax returns quickly and accurately. Apply yourself and you may be in the tax-preparation business in a matter of a few weeks, certainly in time to cash in on the upcoming tax season.

The folks at FTS make it so simple and easy to learn. They have trained thousands of folks with no previous experience—homemakers, truck drivers, retirees, salespeople, office workers, factory workers, sales clerks, teachers, and more.

Tax preparation is a busy, profitable 15-week season! January 1 is when most people start thinking and worrying about taxes, and it's then that the action starts. And it builds through January, February, and March, reaching a peak the first two weeks in April. So, in a short 3 1/2-month tax season, you may earn as much spare-time income as most folks would be happy with for a full year!

Knowing how to prepare tax returns is one thing—but they train you to be an expert. Getting folks in your community to use your service is an entirely different matter. That's where FTS stands tall! You're given practical, down-to-earth help—ads to run, signs to post, business cards to distribute, letters to mail, materials to use—all pointed to getting taxpayers in your community to learn about your service. You're also provided detailed directions to follow so you can begin doing tax returns from your home, for a local store, or from an office. Yes, FTS-trained tax preparers are constantly amazed and pleased with their ongoing success. You will be, too!

For more information, write to

Federated Tax Service
2021 W. Montrose Avenue
Chicago, IL   60618
(800) 621-5199

CREDIT CARD MARKETING TO COLLEGE STUDENTS / Financial Planning Associates

College students usually have a hard time qualifying for credit cards because they have neither established credit, steady income, nor the personal assets major credit card companies such as American Express, Visa, and MasterCard look for.

Those days are over! Financial Planning Associates (FPA) finally cracked the student credit card market by affiliating with one savvy lender that discovered just how profitable credit cards can be in the hands of college students. But to reach the waiting student market, spare-time credit card representatives are needed to process student credit card applications—and make a small bundle in the process!

FPA's lender will instruct you how to set up tables at selected universities in choice locations to market major credit cards—Visa, MasterCard, American Express, Sears, gas company cards, and so forth. Your job is to get as *many* applications as possible filled out each day! And you are paid $2.00–$2.50 and sometimes more for each application you process. It is common for an FPA representative to process 75–150 applications and more per day, so there's money to be made. You can even train students to work for you and you can have five, ten, or more schools operating each day, earning you an override of $1,000–$2,000 or more per week *easily*. Once you join the FPA program, you'll receive an introduction to the lender, complete training manuals and start-up instructions, plus a training cassette tape to help you train agents quickly and easily.

This is an unprecedented money-making opportunity because the vast student market is untapped; college students will gravitate to you like iron filings to a magnet once they learn they can qualify for credit cards. One rep says it is "as easy as raking in the money because that's precisely what this business is."

Work whatever hours you choose. Most FPA reps, however, work two to three days during the week and report excellent incomes (as much as most people earn full-time). Colleges are cooperative because they realize you are helping their students. You can, of course, also market your credit card program through college newspapers and magazines, or even by simple announcements on bulletin boards and fraternity and sorority mailings. However you reach the students, you'll soon be swamped (often with more applications than you can handle), because students *want* credit cards and you are the one individual who can get them the cards they want. This is an ideal opportunity for men and women of any age or background. And the best part is that this is a business you can start for (hold onto your hat) only $150.

There are thousands of colleges and universities with millions of college students enrolled who are your potential customers. And your only job is to make sure that the applications are properly completed and signed. Even if a student is rejected for a credit card (most are approved), you are *still* paid for the properly completed application.

This is one program that offers steady income potential on a continuous basis, and it's one you can enjoy operating no matter what your background may be.

For more information, write to

Financial Planning Associates
210 Fifth Avenue
New York, NY   10010
(718) 768-6803

LOAN MARKETING TO HEALTH CARE PROFESSIONALS / Financial Planning Associates

As you have probably read in your local newspaper or *The Wall Street Journal* or perhaps seen on TV, the health care field is the fastest-growing industry in America today. With the four money-making programs we are now going to tell you about, you can cut yourself a "slice" from this lucrative industry.

People typically think doctors and dentists earn megabuck incomes. Perhaps some do. The reality is that the average doctor earns $126,000 per year (before taxes), and the average dentist grosses only $89,000—according to the Department of Commerce. To effectively compete in the rapidly growing health care market, doctors, dentists, and other health care professionals must now spend great deals of money on advertising, malpractice insurance, new-technology equipment, and expansion costs. To make a long story short, health care professionals need more money than ever before—and their financial dilemma can earn you many thousands of dollars in loan commissions in the weeks and months ahead!

To exploit this demand, Financial Planning Associates (FPA) has developed lending sources that have unlimited funds available for health care professionals (up to $1.2 million per borrower!). FPA has specialized in health care professional loans for the past 15 years. Why?

Because their lenders know doctors have an inflation-proof/recession-proof, almost-guaranteed income. And since they have state licenses to worry about, they rarely lie on a loan application or default on a loan and risk their reputation. Yes, the money they lend is statistically quite safe. This explains why more than 80 percent of all loan submissions are approved, which in turn means 80 percent of your loan submissions result in a fat commission check for you! And since FPA's four financing programs are highly competitive with any loan health care professionals can obtain from local banks, your opportunity to earn big money on these four programs is truly spectacular!

Associated with FPA, you can arrange for health care professionals four widely needed type loans—unsecured loans, 20-year amortized secured loans, equipment sale/leaseback financing, and accounts receivable financing. There's an attractive loan program to interest just about any health care professional you will come in contact with.

Your commission potential is enormous. Arrange a $50,000 equipment loan and you can earn, for example, a 4 percent ($2,000) commission! Other loans can be just as lucrative.

The health care professional market is huge (over a half million health care professionals—and growing) and so will your broker earning potential. You have not only more than 366,000 doctors and 154,000 dentists who need financing, but also 19,500 chiropractors, 22,000 optometrists, 10,500 podiatrists, 18,200 osteopaths, 9,800 opticians, 33,000 veterinarians, plus thousands of other health care professionals. And as you know, every doctor knows dozens of other doctors with similar financing needs, so the referral and word-of-mouth business can be constant!

Meet only 10–12 health professionals a week, tell them about your financing programs, and you're bound to sell at least one financing program. But that *one* sale will put thousands of dollars directly into *your* bank account.

Enroll in this program on either of two levels. You can be an FPA Health Care Professional Loan Representative (only $150) or become a regional director for $495. Call now to see if your area is available, as FPA reports that territories are closing fast.

For more information, write to

**Financial Planning Associates
210 Fifth Avenue
New York, NY   10010
(718) 768-6803**

CONSULTING SERVICES / The Garrett Group

The consulting profession has become an ever-demanding but also ever-profitable business in recent years. According to business experts, economics is the reason for the boom in consulting services: It's cheaper to bring in a consultant to deal with a specific problem than to maintain a full-time staff large enough and versatile enough to cope with every type of crisis.

Unfortunately, the profession has not progressed to the point where everyone understands what a consultant is or what a consultant can do to help management tackle problems. Yet the consulting profession is one of the oldest (no, not the oldest) professions in the world, and the demand for such services are higher than ever.

This is particularly true with The Garrett Group, which specializes in providing consulting services exclusively to financially troubled companies. Garrett is one of the nation's largest and most successful debt restructuring firms, having helped more than 2,000 companies of every size and type of business reduce or eliminate burdensome bank loans, or threatening tax and general creditor claims that cause nightmares for owners of these debt-ridden companies.

More than 8 million small and mid-sized firms suffer severe financial problems, according to Arnold Galahow, Garrett's president. The problem is that most failing companies don't know where to turn for help and, lacking professional guidance, inevitably do fail.

Garrett, like most aggressive consulting firms, also believes in a strong marketing program to find prospective clients. And this can spell opportunity.

The Garrett Group is looking for associate consultants to work with them, locate prospective clients, and also serve as client liaisons. Garrett professionals provide the actual turnaround services, so no special background or training in this complex field is required.

Garrett pays its associate consultants one-third of the fees paid by each client that originates from the associate. Since fees often reach $15,000–$20,000 (and considerably more for a complex workout), the associate consultants routinely earn $5,000–$7,000 for accounts they refer.

Garrett provides two days of training and offers continuous field support and marketing assistance to each of its associate consultants. Garrett maintains regional offices in Boston, Chicago, Rochester, Milwaukee, and Los Angeles, all coordinated from the head office in Florida. Current plans are to actively recruit associate consultants nationwide to reach the tens of thousands of prospective clients in need of Garrett's services.

An associate consultant coordinating services for as few as two to three clients a year can easily earn $300–$500 a week and spend less than 10 hours. No advance fee or investment is required to participate as an associate consultant.

No school or university teaches the various skills needed to be a professional business and management consultant. However, the prerequisites are a good formal education and practical administrative and managerial experience. These special professionals must have an outstanding ability to think and solve problems.

Associates are granted exclusive territories, usually on a statewide basis. The associate attracts clients through classified ads (supplied by Garrett), and through networking with accountants, attorneys, and consultants in other fields. The associate conducts the initial client interview, collecting data and information about the prospective client's problems. This, however, is no more difficult than completing some basic forms. The actual analysis and client assessment are undertaken by Garrett. The subsequent division of responsibility between Garrett and its associates depends on the associates' capabilities. Garrett is particularly interested in recruiting professionals such as attorneys, accountants, and consultants in other management areas who routinely come across prospective clients in their regular practice and who have experience interfacing professionally with clients. Several of these professionals have added tens of thousands of dollars to their existing income.

For more information, write to

The Garrett Group
366 SE 5th Avenue
Delray Beach, FL   33483
(407) 243-3701

976 PHONE SERVICE /
GC Publishing

You've read about it in magazines. You've seen it on television.

This is *the* part-time business that requires no office and no employees, yet can bring in a profit of more than $1,000 a day! And, even better, this payment comes in the form of one big monthly check from the phone company.

We're talking about the amazing new 976 phone business. Working with major phone companies, 976 phone lines bring in literally thousands of calls per month and make their owners up to $1.40 with every call. One 976 owner we talked to makes over a million dollars a year with no direct selling and no special skills—just by selling information that's readily available and in big demand by the public!

These 976 phone lines have become the most promising way for entrepreneurs to cash in on the exploding field of telecommunications. Anyone with information to offer to the public—horoscopes, financial information, employment, news, sports updates, and so on—can sell this information over the phone and make $20,000–$30,000 or more per month.

For example, we located a Cape Cod entrepreneur who gives fishermen daily updates on where the fish are biting. This gem of an idea brings in more than 300 calls every day during the season, and for only five minutes spent updating the phone machine's message each day, this clever entrepreneur earns nearly $500.

There's just *one* problem with this business. Only a few people know the secrets of how to profit from a 976 line. But then we came across *Making a Fortune with 976*, a fascinating guide that reveals all the inside tips to starting your own successful 976 line business. Within this valuable guide you'll discover

- Which 976 lines make the most money
- What advertising ideas work best

- How to buy the equipment you need on a shoestring budget
- How to maximize profits
- The hottest "976" ideas for the 1990s
- And much, much more.

This exclusive guide, written by two of the most successful 976 operators in the country, guarantees to save you countless hours of research and helps you avoid making those costly mistakes in starting your 976 business.

People from all backgrounds and income levels can jump into this lucrative field to launch their own 976 lines. The 976 industry is only just beginning to pick up momentum, and industry experts predict it will quadruple in size within the next two years! So why wait? With little more than a telephone and *Making a Fortune with 976* (only $22.95) at your fingertips, you can be part of this money-making industry tomorrow.

For more information, write to

GC Publishing
12021 Wilshire Blvd. #7063
Los Angeles, CA   90025

BUSINESS SERVICES / General Business Services

Of the 14 million businesses in America, nearly 13 million (or 92 percent) are "small businesses" that need ongoing support services in areas of financial management, basic accounting, tax preparation, and general business consulting.

So where can these businesses turn for help? An increasingly popular answer is General Business Services (GBS), America's largest business service franchise with more than 600 franchises serving tens of thousands of small companies of every size and description.

If you have basic business skills, are well organized and enjoy working with numbers, General Business Services may be an ideal spare-time opportunity; you can usually handle clients during evening or weekend hours or limit your number of clients so you can control the required hours to match your schedule.

What type of services will you provide? You might help a client financially plan a new business or expansion, or perhaps even buy or sell a business. Established businesses will turn to you for basic financial guidance such as the preparation of financial statements, budgets, and tax returns. Depending on your skills, you can provide a far wider range of consulting advice to your clients, and this flexibility can indeed make your affiliation with General Business Services a challenging experience.

Training is the key to the success of GBS. As a GBS franchisee, you receive complete training, continuing support, and the material needed to efficiently service each client using the GBS financial management system. We know of no similar system that provides their franchisees quite the degree of training as GBS, and because professional skills are so important in this business, we rated GBS tops in a very rewarding business.

The GBS franchise fee is $21,500 and additional costs range between $8,000 and $10,000. GBS charges a 7 percent royalty, but no advertising fee.

How much can you earn operating your own GBS office? Income varies, of course, but many GBS representatives report earning more than $60,000 a year full-time. It is possible to earn $20,000-$30,000 working several nights and Saturdays.

There are several competitive business services, but General Business Services is the largest for good reason. Not only is its training program superb, but it is also the best-known service of its type in the business, making it easy for you to attract new clients.

This is a particularly good franchise to consider if you already have a related sideline business but want to expand the scope of your services to include financial services. You not only will expand your client base, but will become much more essential to the success of your client, and thus a more important member of its professional team.

For more information, write to

**General Business Services
20271 Goldenrod Lane
Germantown, MD   20874
(301) 428-1040**

HOME CLEANING AND MAID SERVICE / Guarantee Girls

For the 15 years Ellen Folks has worked in the house-cleaning industry, she watched it become one of the country's five fastest-growing service industries, and for good reason: "More than 60 percent of all households now have two income earners," she said. "And with both people working, who wants to clean house?"

To set her young company apart from other franchises in this burgeoning field, Folks created a three-step plan to diversify her business by adding carpet cleaning and restoration services for homes damaged by fire or water. As she explains, "The franchisees start out by providing the basic house cleaning services, then learn the carpet cleaning business and finally, everything from roof repair to painting and carpentry." According to Folks, home cleaning accounts for the majority of her business, with carpet cleaning and restoration work providing about 20 percent.

Guarantee Girls also differs from other maid service franchises because only two workers are sent out to clean a house, instead of three or four people like most other franchised operations. Folks feels this actually makes the work get done more quickly. Guarantee Girls workers also drive their own cars, a system that cuts overhead expenses and eliminates the need for the franchise to maintain a fleet of cars.

The volume of business done at Folks' store in Baton Rouge, Louisiana is a good indication of the potential offered by a Guarantee Girls franchise: It employs 25 full-time people who clean 200–300 homes per week, for a gross monthly income of approximately $35,000–$45,000. And, it should be noted, this is in a depressed location of 10–12 percent unemployment, so the potential probably would be greater in an area with a higher percentage of two-income families.

Guarantee Girls provides everything the franchisee needs to get started, including enough chemicals and supplies for the first 100 jobs. The one-week training program covers everything from actual house-cleaning techniques to business procedures for answering the phone, scheduling appointments, and bookkeeping skills.

Guarantee Girls requires a $10,000 franchise fee, which includes training. It is recommended that franchisees have an additional $3,000–$5,000 for operating capital during the first few months. This modest investment makes it one of the least costly cleaning franchises available today, and one in which the franchisee can work from his or her home at the beginning.

"For less than the cost of buying a new car, you can get into this fast growing field," Folks says. "And with our emphasis upon diversification, we believe we can thrive in this exciting and intensely competitive market."

Home cleaning will continue to grow in popularity over the next decade, industry experts predict. Because competition is keen, there is great need for services to develop competitive advantages if they are to succeed. We believe the Guarantee Girls will become increasingly stronger as a market contender because it recognizes this fact—and is constantly in search of new and important ways to set its service apart from others and to provide better customer service.

You can start your Guarantee Girls business on a spare-time basis and easily grow into a full-time venture as your clientele expands. Many operators in this industry *net* $1,000 a week or more running their business full-time, with proportionately less income with reduced hours.

There are many interesting franchises in this field, and although it's still a new entrant, we believe we've found a winner with the Guarantee Girls.

For more information, write to

Guarantee Girls
6210 Hollyfield Drive
Baton Rouge, LA   70810
(800) 735-4475

CHILDREN'S FITNESS CENTERS / Gymboree

With a baby boom currently in progress, it's only logical that the fitness craze encompass children as well as adults. That's the reasoning behind Gymboree, which began in 1976 as a local exercise program for California tots and now boasts almost 200 successful franchises throughout the United States and Canada.

Joan Barnes, president and creator of Gymboree, originally created the concept because "I couldn't find an activity where parents and preschoolers could play together." Using her background as a recreation adviser, Barnes launched a development program for tots involving motor skills, sensory perceptions, games, songs, and play. Mothers told other mothers, Barnes trained teachers, and eventually a booming franchise system was well on its way.

Gymboree begins with babies at just three months of age and progresses to specially designed activities for preschoolers. Each Gymboree site has about 40 colorful pieces of play equipment, including balance beams, ladders, slides, tunnels, and other toys to stimulate muscles, joints, and senses. Parents pay $50–$60 for 12 weekly sessions, and must accompany their small fry to class.

Gymboree has turned out to be a breeding ground for female executives. All but four of the 25 corporate employees are women. And by coincidence rather than design, all franchises are owned by women or couples, many of whom are former special education teachers or homemakers. Franchise applicants are rigorously screened and must travel to Gymboree's Burlingame, California headquarters for a comprehensive training program. Company reps also visit franchises regularly, and annual meetings are held to both review and plan operations.

Gymboree rarely enters a market of less than 100,000 population, and franchisees are usually required to buy a minimum of two centers, with exclusive territorial rights guaranteed. Each franchise costs about $10,000–$14,000 depending on location, and equipment adds another $8,000 to the total start-up costs. Operators pay the company a 6 percent monthly royalty. Because classes are held in rented space in YMCAs, churches, or community centers, no real estate investment is necessary. To help spread the word, a syndicated column called "Gymboree" appears in almost 300 newspapers, and a Gymboree home video and a line of toys and clothes are soon to be launched, further perpetuating the Gymboree name among households with tots.

Gymboree is a business that demands commitment on the part of its franchisees because they not only must learn the Gymboree system, but must also be prepared to spend a fixed number of hours per week with the enrolled tots. Yet this does not require a full-time effort. You can operate your Gymboree in the morning and still have plenty of time for yourself during the afternoon and evening. Although it's difficult to estimate earnings potential, the sly smile of several Gymboree owners suggests an answer.

What will it take to *really* succeed in this business? A love for children. But if you enjoy surrounding yourself with a band of happy kids, then Gymboree can be just the business you're looking for.

For more information, write to

Gymboree
872 Hinckley Road
Burlingame, CA   94010
(415) 579-0600

SHOE SALES / Hanover Shoe Co.

When you think of buying shoes, you usually think of traveling to your local shoe store. But Hanover Shoes has proven just how profitable it can be to bring the shoes to the customer.

Hanover Shoes has been making quality footwear since 1899 while offering its products directly to the consumer through an independent sales organization since 1963. A wide range of sizes and widths in both men's and ladies' styles is offered. The distribution center contains more than 750,000 pairs of shoes in sizes that range from 6 to 15 and widths from AA to EEEE. No retail store can offer such a wide selection, and Hanover prides itself on the fact that there are shoes for every taste, purpose, size, and pocketbook.

Anyone who enjoys interacting with people will find the Hanover program very appealing. The need for this source of difficult-to-find sizes and widths gives you the opportunity to satisfy the needs of a vast majority of the buying public. Information to start your business is available in Hanover's *free* starter kit. Field training with an established sales representative is available on request in select areas.

Since you are independent, your earning income is controlled solely by your own efforts. Average commission per pair is about $10. Some reps who have developed their business as a profitable full-time business are consistently earning $30,000 to $40,000 a year.

The amount of time devoted to this business opportunity depends on the individual. Historically Hanover's sales reps have earned $10 plus per hour of selling effort, but some earn $30–$40, particularly if they have an established customer base and can benefit from repeat sales.

As a Hanover representative you carry no inventory (except perhaps a sample pair to show the fine quality of the Hanover shoe). The company drop-ships to all customers, so you can devote your time to generating profitable sales.

In addition to a steady income, there are a number of additional benefits from becoming a Hanover representative. You can earn *free* shoes (think how much you can save on shoes for you and your family) and earn override payments. You also enjoy the opportunity to participate in periodic contests with generous prizes. Most importantly, you can qualify for health and life insurance. You can even increase earnings by referring others to the Hanover opportunity.

Hanover shoes sell exceptionally well because they represent real value. Moreover, you can offer so many types of shoes, sizes, and styles not easily found in shoe stores.

As a Hanover rep you can even recruit salespeople to work under you. This gives you the opportunity to build a sales empire of your own! Best of all, you have absolutely *no investment* as a Hanover rep.

Hanover shoes are easy to sell. Many reps successfully sell on a door-to-door basis, but this shoe line can also be sold through parties, or in combination with a related product.

Why not try selling Hanover shoes to your relatives and friends? You'll see how easy it is to get the ball rolling.

For more information, write to

Hanover Shoe Co.
Dept. 4032
118 Carlisle Street
Hanover, PA   17331
(717) 632-7575
Contact: Robert Peiffer

DRIVEWAY SEALING / Harrington Driveway Sealing

Cruise around your community and you'll probably find 50 percent or more of the asphalt driveways in need of blacktopping right now! Then think of how many of those homeowners could be sold a blacktopping service that is both superior in quality and lower in cost than conventional services.

Driveways need blacktopping every two or three years to look attractive. Untreated, they discolor and develop unsightly cracks and small holes.

The problem is that homeowners must turn to large commercial firms to repair their driveways, and such services simply aren't geared for the residential market (most concentrate on commercial installations), and as a result are overpriced.

Enter Harrington Driveway Sealing.

What makes Harrington Driveway Sealing unique is that it services the residential market *exclusively*. This means faster and more economical service. It also means targeted marketing necessary to more effectively reach the homeowner market. More importantly, Harrington has an exclusive blacktop coating additive to significantly improve the durability of the coating so Harrington driveways stay attractively sealed two or three times longer than those conventionally coated.

Harrington's blacktopping business has been so successful in Cincinnati, where the process originated, it is now franchising its system nationwide.

You can become part of this rapidly growing field with a phone call to Harrington. But book fast. Franchises *are* selling! If accepted, you'll undergo complete training (the special process is easily learned) and have the benefit of fast sales from the professional marketing program to instantly hand you the lion's share of the driveway repair business in your neighborhood.

Expect top earnings as part of the Harrington team. You can easily blacktop five to six driveways a day (at $150 an average job in most areas) and take home $1,000 after expenses. Your customers will enjoy a great-looking driveway, one that will stay beautiful for years to come. This is indeed a win–win situation.

Harrington can tailor your investment to match the equipment you need. (If you already own a truck, for example, your start-up costs will be exceptionally small.)

Discover what's in driveway sealing for you. Work part-time and earn $50,000 a year. And you won't find the work difficult to learn or to handle.

This is a nonseasonal, all-area, repeat business. Demand is constant—and customers are exceptionally easy to find. All you need do is cruise your neighborhood.

You can begin your blacktopping business part-time. In fact, the best hours of operation are weekends because you can most easily sign up jobs when most homeowners are home from work. And with the Harrington name behind you, resistance is low because customers need not fear a scam or rip-off that has hurt this industry badly.

A recognized name, superior quality, low price, high profits. With this combination, Harrington's can be to asphalt blacktopping what McDonald's is to hamburgers.

For more information, write to

Harrington Driveway Sealing
26 E. 6th Street
Cincinnati, OH   45201
(513) 421-0444
Contact: Charles Harrington

SYNTHETIC GEMSTONES /
Harris Marketing

What do "Dynasty," "Falcon Crest," "The Love Boat," "Beverly Hills Cop," and "Rocky IV" have in common? No, you'll never guess. The answer is that their stars all wear exquisite (but ridiculously inexpensive) jewelry known as Our Secret Creations and marketed exclusively through Harris Marketing Distributors.

But you don't have to be a movie or TV star to enjoy these cubic zirconia and artificial gemstones beautiful enough to convince a master jeweler they are the real thing. Your friends and neighbors will want the same sense of luxury as so many celebrities who proudly wear these "undetectable from diamond" gemstones.

The market for synthetic jewelry is growing by leaps and bounds. Real diamonds have lost their glitter as investments, and who can afford the high insurance costs for expensive jewelry? So the answer for most people is to buy the look of diamonds at a small fraction of the real price. Based on that exciting concept, Our Secret Creations now has over 700 successful distributors from coast to coast racking up record sales and profits.

You too can be a successful distributor. Sell the Our Secret Creations line in 101 different ways—through retail or wholesale sales, at parties, or as corporate bonuses or premiums, to mention a few of the more popular methods.

To succeed you need basic business skills, but more importantly you must be a motivated salesperson with a positive attitude and good follow-up. Harris Marketing offers all the support you'll need with extensive initial training as well as ongoing training programs.

Earnings are unlimited, with many distributors earning more than $1,000 a week part-time. Best of all, start-up costs are surprisingly low. Only $475 brings you a starter kit complete with exquisite samples. We challenge you and your friends to compare and distinguish Our Secret Creations from real gems.

Our Secret Creations is an exceptionally terrific line if you are already selling through party plans (cosmetics, lingerie, and so forth). Jewelry is a natural seller when coupled with related products.

Our Secret Creations offers not only the most realistic gemstone facsimiles available on the market today, but the widest selection as well. And that's precisely why we picked Our Secret Creations for *100 Best*. In reaching this industry, we discovered selection is the key to success, and no company offers a greater selection (and business-building potential) than the folks at Our Secret Creations.

For more information, write to

Harris Marketing & Associates
P.O. Box 8175
Cincinnati, OH   45208
(513) 871-4987
Contact: Pamela Slutzky

REAL ESTATE PUBLICATION / Homestead Publications

How would you like to be a successful publisher of real estate listings available from local brokers in your area?

Homestead Publications, Inc. is nothing less than a publishing revolution. Although Homestead Publications, Inc. has been operating successfully for a number of years now, management realized that success would always be limited unless a way was found to tap into the enormous nationwide market for their quality specialized printing products. Enter the unique concept of associate publishers! By placing carefully selected and specially trained entrepreneurs in protected territories, tremendous access to the thousands of real estate brokers throughout the entire country is now possible. This mutually beneficial system allows associate publishers to concentrate on making a great deal of money by working with the brokers, while at the same time allowing Homestead Publications, Inc. to stay in its national headquarters concentrating on what it does best—producing high-quality, specialized printing! In fact, Homestead Publications, Inc. even has its very own art department, in-house computer typesetting system, and state-of-the-art printing presses.

The market starts with the tens of thousands of real estate brokers nationwide. Each broker deals with many related businesses and services, and every one of these is a potential customer for your new business. The reason you can enjoy a cooperative relationship with real estate brokers is that like all good businesspeople, brokers constantly want to improve the image of their business.

Although your business begins with contacting various real estate brokers, your profits will not come directly from them, but rather from the many businesses and service companies associated with these brokers. For example, consider such businesses as general contractors, electricians, movers, exterminators, landscapers, rubbish removals, surveyors, truck renters, banks, interior designers, locksmiths, insulation contractors, insurance companies, plumbers, home security specialists, and hundreds of other home-related operations. These businesses and services depend on broker referrals for much of their income, and they understand the importance of mutual cooperation and support so that everyone can enjoy a prosperous business environment.

Although no previous experience is required, some background in management, sales, real estate, or advertising can be helpful. A training program has been developed that can teach you everything you need to know in order to succeed. However, Homestead cannot do the actual work for you. It is your determination to succeed that must drive you to work hard for the substantial rewards this profitable business can offer.

When its unique publishing system was created, Homestead Publications, Inc. decided its profit would only come from the quality printing it does for its associate publishers, and not from unreasonable sky-high franchise fees. The low $495 initial investment covers advertising and related costs in finding and developing associate publishers. For that fee you will receive training which includes a confidential sales manual, sample publications, and free telephone access to experienced Homestead Publications, Inc. consultants. You will also have the opportunity to expand your business through new products and services offered exclusively to associate publishers, and, of course, exclusive access to the amazing high-quality personalized production available only through Homestead Publications, Inc.

Because associate publishers are selected and awarded protected territories on a first-come, first-served basis, it is critically important for you to act now for your best chance at this most exciting opportunity, if you feel you indeed possess the necessary qualifications to achieve success in this highly profitable and rapidly expanding business.

If you are accepted and join the team, you will find Homestead dedicated, motivated, and committed to your success. After all, your success relates directly to its success! Indeed, today Homestead Publications, Inc. is fortunate in having associate publishers with incomes of more than $1,000 a week. Perhaps you can be one!

For more information, write to

Homestead Publications, Inc.
411 Commerce Lane
Berlin, NJ   08009
(609) 753-9713

WATER PURIFIER SYSTEMS / Hurley Chicago Co.

Caution: The water you drink may be hazardous to your health.

According to Gus Losos, president of Hurley Chicago Co., there is much disagreement in scientific circles as to the extent of risk to prolonged exposure to deadly chemicals in ordinary drinking water, some of which are dangerous in low concentrations such as are measured as parts per billion.

Losos claims his company's Granular Activated Carbon Systems water filtration units are similar to the highly acclaimed water treatment equipment that effectively treated trichloroethane and perchloroethylene contamination in the town of Rockaway Borough, New Jersey. "When the GAC was put into operation, the TCE and PCE levels dropped to non-detectable amounts."

Losos is actively seeking distributors who are acquainted with direct sales and who wish to become part of the Hurley family. In 1979 there were ten active distributors; presently there are more than 300 in the United States and 16 overseas, so you can see what a growth opportunity this is.

It's obvious that the market for water treatment and conditioning products will continue its explosive growth. More and more homeowners are in the market for water-purification systems. Many cities and towns are even warning citizens about the dangers of drinking untreated municipal water, encouraging homeowners to install their own purification systems as an essential health measure. A little foresight now about water problems on the part of direct salespeople can lead to a great income later as the water-purification field continues to grow!

Surprisingly, only 7 percent of U.S. homes presently have some kind of water-filtration system. The remaining 93 percent are waiting for you to ask for their order. In addition to the residential market, there is an enormous commercial market that shares the same need for an effective and economical water-filtration system.

Hurley Chicago dealers typically are ambitious and motivated self-starters who have direct sales experience and know-how or can be trained to manage a dealer and sales organization.

As a dealer you have open territories and will undergo a comprehensive training program (including Hurley's proven sales presentation). There are plenty of orders waiting to be processed, so your earnings are limited only by your effort and the number of hours you choose to work.

Water purification is an exceptionally profitable business. You can earn sizable commissions on each system sold and begin today with absolutely no investment on your part. Some Hurley representatives earn several hundred dollars a week selling on a spare-time basis. Income is steady and can only grow as the market increasingly turns to water-purification systems as a necessary prevention to the dangers of their present water supply.

For more information, write to

Hurley Chicago Co., Inc.
12621 South Laramie Avenue
Alsip, IL   60658
(312) 388-9222

INVENTION PROCESSING / Invention Submission Corporation

What could be more fun and challenging than helping entrepreneurs turn their new products into money makers? Act now and you *can* work with aspiring inventors, authors, and entrepreneurs as part of Invention Submission Corporation (ISC), America's largest and most complete invention services organization.

ISC has helped hundreds of entrepreneurs capitalize on their inventions by properly packaging the invention to industry. ISC negotiates licensing and distribution rights and also provides supplementary marketing services to entrepreneurs who want to market their products on their own. ISC also provides a complete subsidy publishing program for authors.

Here's how you can fit into the ISC organization. ISC attracts entrepreneurs with products to license through extensive newspaper and magazine advertising. It also sponsors a national trade show for inventions (INPEX). Prospective clients in your area are referred directly to you. Your function is to initially process clients, applications and then participate with ISC in fulfilling the services to the client. You share what are often very lucrative fees on a 50–50 basis with ISC.

An ISC sales office can be started in any metropolitan area for very little capital. There are no franchise fees or other up-front payments. Training is free. You can start your office out of an existing business office or rent an inexpensive furnished office. You never need to travel; clients come to you.

In addition to your 50 percent commission, you can also earn a hefty monthly sales incentive bonus.

This is an excellent part-time opportunity for a businessperson, sales rep, business broker, insurance or real estate agent, teacher, or any other "people-oriented" person with follow-through and an enthusiasm for new ideas.

You can easily market your services with small classified ads, through direct solicitation to entrepreneurs with interesting products, or by conducting seminars for people with products in the start-up stage. Prospective authors can be attracted with brochures distributed at local writing courses. There is an endless list of proven ways to come together with people who need ISC's important services.

No previous business or legal experience is necessary to excel in this business because the technical work is handled by ISC. You do need "people" skills—the ability to gain client confidence, to understand client objectives, and to work cooperatively with ISC so clients' needs are handled efficiently and professionally.

This can be a rewarding sideline business. Some deals involving new products involve tens of thousands of dollars in fees. Your 50 percent commissions can really add up over the course of a year.

For more information, write to

Invention Submission Corporation
903 Liberty Avenue
Pittsburgh, PA   15222
(412) 288-1300

JANITORIAL SERVICE /
Jani-King International, Inc.

The commercial cleaning field, in big, big demand, is also the *one* business not affected by interest rates, supply shortages, or style changes. What the field is desperately short of are the qualified people now needed to handle everyday janitorial work for small offices and other commercial businesses.

That's why Jani-King dealers are in exceptionally high demand by prospective clients. And the folks at Jani-King are called first when janitorial services are needed, because they have the image and reputation of size, strength, dependability, stability, and leadership in the commercial cleaning industry. In fact, Jani-King has been an industry leader since 1969, so you start with a highly experienced name behind you.

The franchise is sold under five different plans. The lowest priced plan, Plan A, is $6,500; the highest priced plan is Plan E, which is $14,000 plus. All plans except Plan A guarantee the new franchise owner a specified amount of annual business from $12,000 to $36,000 or more.

Jani-King offers a well-structured, extensively researched program for building financial security from monthly cleaning contracts. Its system has been proven by franchisees nationwide.

As part of the Jani-King team you receive professional, thorough training and continued guidance. The professional staff provides continuing support and assistance in securing and managing new business and keeping building clients satisfied.

For their investment the franchisees receive a specified amount of monthly accounts and supplies and equipment. Jani-King also provides the franchise owner with partial financing of their franchise fee. Training and back-up services such as marketing and sales support, billing, and cleaning supply research are also a part of a Jani-King franchise. In return, the franchise owner agrees to pay a 10 percent royalty on his gross monthly revenues. All franchises are insured and bonded.

This is a business you can start part-time and can gradually expand into a full-time business. You can earn between $300 and $600 a week part-time, and far more if you want to supervise multiple crews. And best of all, you don't have to perform janitorial work yourself, but can supervise crews and sell new accounts.

The program seems to be working. Jani-King has sold more than 1,400 franchises in the United States and Canada. Those franchises had $40 million in total billings in 1988. *Entrepreneur* magazine recently (1988) ranked Jani-King the number one franchise in its industry and the 26th franchise in the United States (out of over 500) in its annual Franchise 500 issue.

Jani-King theory is that highly motivated owner-managers provide the best service.

For more information, write to

Jani-King International, Inc.
4950 Keller Springs, Suite 190
Dallas, TX   75248
(800) 552-5264
In Texas: (800) 533-9406

JEWELRY FASHION ADVISER / Lady Remington

More than 3,000 successful fashion advisers now sell the famous Lady Remington fashion jewelry line through party plans.

Why should you become a Lady Remington Fashion Adviser?

If we said "To make extra money," we'd be right, but we'd be giving you only part of the story. Making money is a very important part, to be sure, because with Lady Remington you can make *very* good money with practically no effort and using very little of your spare time.

But many Remington people tell us they find other benefits that are just as important. For instance, having fun in what they are doing ranks high. Lady Remington shows are a lot of fun. You play games, meet new people, chat, learn what's going on. And it's a chance to get out and do something different—work that's a change of pace from the everyday "hum-drum."

You'd be surprised at the backgrounds of most Lady Remington Fashion Advisers. Secretaries, homemakers, waitresses, clerks, schoolteachers, you name it—they come from every walk of life. By and large, they have never sold anything before in their lives, and perhaps the only thing they knew about jewelry is that "diamonds are a girl's best friend." They also know that they wear jewelry and they like it, and they sell jewelry and like it. The main qualification for being a Lady Remington adviser? A few hours a week you can spare—and the desire to succeed with the Lady Remington opportunity.

It won't cost you a penny to start. Lady Remington starts you out with a packed sample kit containing approximately $700 worth of glittering jewelry, plus lots of extra materials that will help you build your business fast. You earn your sample kit with your first $150 in commissions, and then everything in your kit is yours.

Why did we select Lady Remington as one of the *100 Best*?

There are two good reasons. First, because so many women love to wear fine jewelry, and when they can buy the best at "lower than jewelry store prices," they find it difficult to resist. Second, because the Lady Remington shows are so much fun to sponsor. The Lady Remington name and all it stands for have become so popular a social event, you'll soon find yourself lining up dates for shows weeks and even months in advance.

Work as few or as many hours as you choose. You can easily earn $25-$35 per hour (many advisers earn spectacular six-figure incomes full-time) with the Lady Remington line.

Lady Remington (and its feisty founder, Victor Kiam) stand behind you all the way. Not only does the firm arm you with the finest jewelry available in its price range, but it also fortifies you with a power-packed marketing program to bring you ready, willing, and even ecstatic customers day after day.

Three thousand successful Lady Remington fashion advisers can't be wrong. Lady Remington must be doing something right.

For more information, write to

Lady Remington Fashion Jewelry
Dept. BK
818 Thorndale
Bensenville, IL   60106
(312) 860-3323
Contact: John Kiple

LASER PRINTER CARTRIDGE REFILLS /
Laser Product Consultants

More than 10 million toner cartridges will be consumed and thrown away in 1990. The cost to buy a new cartridge ranges from $90 to $129. In contrast, a refilled toner cartridge is generally priced between $45 and $59. The cost savings per year per customer averages more than $500 when refilled cartridges are used. There are an additional 50,000 new customers in the United States every month as new printers are sold. Each of these printers will also use an average of 5–10 cartridges per year. As customers become more aware of the availability of re-manufactured toner cartridges and of the possible cost savings, many will choose less-costly remanufactured cartridges as op-posed to purchasing new cartridges and throwing their good money away.

Here's another opportunity to think about. Laser printers also require maintenance. Basic preventative maintenance such as cleaning is often overlooked in a busy office. Thus, when the initial manufacturer's warranty has run out, many printers be-come neglected. Two- and three-year-old printers now require new parts on a frequent basis. A service call from the manufac-turer's warranty center will cost about $350. Instead, you can replace and repair worn parts for a fraction of what manufac-turers charge (and can still make a very healthy profit). Both of these money-making opportunities are yours as a Laser Product Consultants dealer.

Laser Product Consultants specializes in remanufacturing cartridges for printers. Although there are more than 400 dealers worldwide, only 5–7 percent of this burgeoning market is being adequately serviced. In addition to toner cartridges, your customers' computer printers may also require the low-cost preventative maintenance and repair program. To handle the enormous volume, Laser Product Consultants is now offering a "full-service" program to dealers. Dealers can supply their customers with preventative maintenance and printer cleaning, and on-site repair service, as well as sell high-quality remanufactured toner cartridges.

This unique program allows dealers to compete more effectively with local shops while providing their customers with tremendous cost savings, top-quality products, and the competent, knowledgeable service that can come only from dealing with masters of the trade.

Dealers are supplied with full training, wholesale supplies, tools and equipment, telephone support, and marketing consultation—everything you need to get into and stay in this exciting business.

Earnings are unlimited. For instance, one remanufactured cartridge can be sold to a customer for $45. The cost of supplies for the cartridge is about $10. Your profit per cartridge is about $35 (not including labor and overhead costs). If you remanufacture 100 cartridges a month, you earn $3,500! And many remanufacturing companies are processing 500–1,000 cartridges per month, so visualize the earnings that can be yours.

And you can make money fast. Four to six cartridges can be remanufactured in less than one hour. A laser printer can be cleaned in about 20 minutes. This explains why some dealers operate only a few hours a week, and others go into business full-time—so they can make even more.

This is a booming business. Whereas at one time every office had typewriters, now offices have personal computers hooked into laser printers and dot matrix printers. Since laser printers are far quieter, print better, and are much easier to use than dot matrix printers, they are a very desirable addition to any workplace. As the cost of laser printers drops (the price has dropped in half in three years), more and more companies are investing in laser printers. Naturally, as the customer base expands, so will your profit potential.

You can literally start this business on a shoestring. The folks at Laser Product Consultants can tell you how easy it is to become one of their successful dealers. But take it from us—you need neither technical skills nor great sales ability to prosper in this business. What you do need is a comprehensive program that delivers to your customers total, low-priced service to keep their printers working.

For more information, write to

Laser Product Consultants
4320 196th Street SW, Suite B-643
Lynnwood, WA   98036
(206) 776-6765

JEWELRY CHAINS / Lasting Impressions, Inc.

One of the hottest marketing concepts of the decade is custom-made (while you wait) quality fashion neck, wrist, and ankle chains. This is one money-making idea that promises to be even hotter in the years to come.

The entire business takes just 30 inches of counter space, yet it can produce whopping profits of 1,500 percent!

A leader in the field is Lasting Impressions (Chains-by-the-Inch). As a Chains-by-the-Inch dealer, you will sell one of the most beautiful assortment of jewelry chains found anywhere in America. The Lasting Impressions line has more than 40 different gold chains (and even bracelets) in perfect 14K color. But unlike other companies who feature only gold chains, Chains-by-the-Inch offers a complete range of other jewelry chains and related jewelry items for every taste. The "Excitement-by-the-Inch" line, for example, features stunning genuine handset cubic zirconia rings. Also, in addition to Chains-by-the-Inch, the company features "Crystals-by-the-Inch," "Rainbows-by-the-Inch," and "Sterling-Layered-by-the-Inch." Yes, you'll have a chain to dazzle every taste.

No special training is required to operate this fantastic business. Anyone and everyone, from teenagers to retired folks, can successfully own and operate this business. Lasting Impressions provides you with full instructions to carefully explain everything you need to know for successfully operating your Chains-by-the-Inch business, so your success is never left to chance.

The entire start-up cost of the business (including a mirrored lucite display, tools, ruler, and inventory) is just $349 complete! For fast delivery, you can even charge your start-up costs to American Express, Visa, or MasterCard.

We selected this as an ideal spare-time business because Chains-by-the-Inch is a natural seller at flea markets, swap meets, fairs, malls, special events, and home parties. If you are already in business selling jewelry, gift items, or related merchandise, you'll find Chains-by-the-Inch one line you will quickly want to add to your existing lines.

Chains-by-the-Inch practically sells itself. Your inventory is easy to keep, inexpensive to buy, and profitable to sell. Each spool of chain offers an endless variety of lengths, so there's no need to stock different-size chains. Simply cut the chain to fit the customer.

Jewelry chains have become a big business. People of every age and sex wear chains. Neck chains, ankle chains, wrist chains—chains are the most popular jewelry. With Chains-by-the-Inch, they have become even more popular because now they can have quality, variety, and low price all in once. That's why Chains-by-the-Inch is so successful. Customers don't buy just one, but several, for a full jewelry assortment for every wardrobe.

Most Chains-by-the-Inch dealers work only a few hours on weekends and still report exceptional earnings, often exceeding $100 an hour in profits. The high-profit potential and small investment make this one opportunity you will want to investigate.

For more information, write to

Lasting Impressions, Inc.
P.O. Box 22065
Lake Buena Vista, FL   32830
(407) 298-5866

REAL ESTATE TAX REDUCTION SERVICE / Lear McNally Corp.

The tax rebellion is here, and the local property tax reduction business is blossoming into one of the most lucrative low-cost opportunities today! How large is it? Just look at the buildings that surround you, factor in the number of possible errors in tax assessment, and you can see a potential that is indeed limitless. The National Taxpayers' Association suggests that 60 percent of all property is overassessed but only a small percentage are actually challenged, so the market is endless.

The problem of inaccurate and inequitable real estate property tax assessment is a serious consumer crisis demanding immediate action. For residential and commercial taxpayers who are unknowingly and needlessly giving away their money, Lear McNally provides timely relief through an exciting service with astonishing profit potential: professional real estate tax reduction.

This service has the potential to benefit anyone who is paying too much real estate tax. Businesses. Commercial and industrial properties. Investors. Your neighbors. These markets each want and need this service for three powerful reasons:

- *Tax reduction saves them money and protects their investment.* As real estate taxes escalate, they are becoming more and more a burden to taxpayers. Many individuals are desperate to the point of selling their properties to escape high real estate taxes.
- *The knowledge to provide this service is known to very few people.* Knowledge is power. And the expertise necessary to provide tax reduction is a very rare commodity in our nation. Therefore, competition for this service is nil.

- *Tax reduction sells itself.* In most cases, tax reduction is offered to clients on a contingency (percentage of savings) basis. For example, your fee could be 50 percent of the taxpayer's first-year savings, plus 25 percent of savings in subsequent years. The client risks nothing and stands to gain tremendously by enlisting your services. The result is a dramatic win–win situation: Your client pays less real estate tax while you earn a substantial fee. Can you imagine an easier "sale" than one that requires no up-front cost to the prospect?

How much money can you make? Your personal wealth has the potential to skyrocket as you build your clientele, and receive residuals for your past cases as well!

Lear McNally forges a long-term commitment to your success by making you an associate in the firm. This means that after your intensive workshop session at corporate offices, your relationship is only beginning. The program gives you the benefit of the company's knowledge, resources, and energetic support to help you build your personal wealth. No specific skills are required. Your success is limited only by your own commitment in time and effort.

This is an ideal spare-time (or full-time) opportunity, and one you can do quite well with working a suggested minimum of ten hours a week.

The business potential speaks for itself, but more specifically its best asset is the low cost of start-up and the fact that you're providing a service that requires no inventory or receivables and has exceptionally low overhead. You may choose to have or not to have employees depending on your goals and objectives. With Lear McNally providing training and support, the real benefit is that you need not "reinvent the wheel" and can drastically reduce the learning curve for start-up time, bringing you that much closer to those big profits. Your investment in this unique business? Only $6,900.

For more information, write to

Lear McNally Corp.
260 S. Broad Street
Philadelphia, PA   19102
(800) 227-7289
In Pennsylvania: (215) 790-0500

MINIATURE GOLF /
Lomma Enterprises, Inc.

What do Walt Disney, Bill Cosby, and Ralph Lomma have in common? By focusing on family fun, they each generate record incomes for their companies and their supporters.

In fact, Ralph Lomma's Lomma Enterprises, Inc., through its design and prefabricated construction of miniature golf courses, has been catering to family fun for generations—and has become a "hole in one" for entrepreneurs ready to cash in from the miniature golf craze.

"Baby Boomers, many of whom probably had one of their first dates playing miniature golf, are now back playing again, this time with their children in tow," states Gary Knight, Lomma Enterprises executive vice-president. "Today's parents feel guilty just 'plopping' down in front of the television set with their children," Knight reminds us. "Others, of course, go into 'ticket shock' after spending an afternoon (and half a day's wages) to see a movie. In a sense, an afternoon or evening playing miniature golf is refreshingly viewed as 'quality time'. Families are not just sitting there being entertained; they are outside, actively involved with each other, entertaining themselves," Knight explains.

Not only is miniature golf wholesome fun, it is also affordable entertainment.

"The entire family—mom, dad, brother, sister, and even grandmother and grandpa can play a round of golf for about the cost of just one admission to a movie. The economy—as well as the challenge of miniature golf—brings them back again and again," Knight says.

Knight speaks from experience. Lomma Enterprises has been making miniature golf courses for 35 years. The courses are in virtually every state in the union as well as overseas. For less than the cost of a new automobile, people are starting their own highly profitable miniature golf business.

Lomma's customized golf courses, which can fit in as small a space as 3,000 square feet, are designed with the family in mind. We all know that children—and their parents—get bored easily. But, since Lomma golf courses are portable with interchangeable parts, the entire course can be rearranged in an hour or so. It continuously gives the course a new and more challenging look. "In what other business can you, at virtually no cost to yourself, give your business a whole new look and feel in an hour or so?" Knight asks.

Lomma officials proudly proclaim that their miniature golf courses have been installed in virtually every type of facility, such as a school in Pennsylvania, a rooftop and boardwalk in New Jersey, a basement in New York, and even on three great cruise ships.

A complete and concise installation of a Lomma golf course is available to you wherever you choose to locate it. However, unlike other companies, it is provided with no royalty or franchise fees.

Because miniature golf is a noninventory, noncommodity business, all cash revenues stay with you. Operators of courses are basically renting "air" and don't have inventory to replace.

Since a great deal of business is done in the evenings and on weekends, a Lomma miniature golf course can be ideal as a spare-time opportunity and an excellent second source of income. And an indoor location can assure you year-round play—and year-round income—regardless of the weather.

What will it cost to start your own Lomma miniature golf course? As little as $8,900. (And remember, there are no franchise fees or royalties to pay—ever!) What can you earn? Receipts of $100,000 a year and up are quite common, and because overhead is exceptionally low, you can take home a sizable week's pay from a business that's fun and easy to operate, and guaranteed to give you a "hole-in-one" toward your future success!

For more information, write to

Lomma Enterprises, Inc.
1120 S. Washington Avenue
Scranton, PA   18505
(717) 346-5559
Contact: Gary Knight

DROP-SHIP MAIL ORDER / Mail Order Associates Inc.

Do you want to cash in on the mail-order boom but say you can't afford to put together that all-important sales tool known as the catalog? And you say you don't have the funds to purchase or the space to stock inventory?

Don't despair. Drop-ship is here and can be your ticket to mail-order success.

The drop-ship method of mail order enables you to become a mail-order entrepreneur without the hassles of

- Producing a catalog
- Acquiring inventory
- Stocking inventory
- Making trips to the post office to ship goods to your mail-order customers.

With drop-ship you simply take orders, deduct your share of the profits, and simply forward the order with appropriate payment and a shipping label to your mail-order product source: the drop-shipper.

The drop-shipper—usually a product manufacturer or wholesale distributor—in turn packs the order and ships it to your customer with the label you've provided. The customer receives the order with your label so assumes it came directly from your company.

Most drop-shippers provide you with free promotional and advertising support in the way of ad slicks, fliers on different products, and sometimes even a full-color catalog with the name of your company emblazoned on the cover, so your job is made even easier.

Mail Order Associates is the leading drop-shipper in the mail-order field. Here's a roundup of how the firm can help put you in your own successful mail-order business literally overnight. Here's how it works. First, the company charges $245 (Visa and MasterCard accepted) to enroll you as a charter member in its fast-growing organization.

But in exchange for that small sum, Mail Order Associates provides you with the following:

- A programmed mail-order course
- Your own mail-order catalogs
- Free samples of products
- Mail-order ads prepared free of charge
- New-products newsletter
- Directories and mailing lists
- Photos of new products
- Trade reports and free consultation.

Beautifully prepared, the Mail Order Associates full-color catalog of about 50 pages contains hundreds of tempting products bargain-priced from $4.95 to $395.00 There's even a special "Bargain Hunters'" section where four hit products may be purchased for only $4.95.

Distribute the catalogs to your mailing list, take a few additional ads on special items you feel will appeal to that audience, and watch the orders roll in! To process the orders, simply deduct your hefty profit and send the shipping label on to the company—and you're ready for the next batch of money in your mailbox.

Average markup for the current product line is a whopping 120 percent. A $44 retail sale will cost your new mail-order company $20, with a generous $24 profit.

Best of all, Mail Order Associates puts you in the mail-order business even if you're on a shoestring budget.

This highly-successful company, founded by master merchandiser Gil Turk, has been in operation for more than 30 years, so it knows this business. Turk, a self-made mail-order millionaire, has successfully sold everything from vitamins and plant food to gifts and accessories through the mail. Like many who want to jump on the mail-order bandwagon, Turk started with virtually no money. His files are full of testimonials from successful mail-order venturers who became charter members of Mail Order Associates and, using his techniques, began pulling in thousands of dollars in extra income per month.

Mail order is the ideal business to start at home, during your spare time. You can begin on a "shoestring"—even while holding your present job. No previous experience is needed. If you are serious and ambitious—eager to build a business of your own—this is the opportunity you've been looking for! Take your first big step toward financial independence, and a chance to make a Mail Order Fortune—far beyond your fondest dreams!

Just as McDonald's restaurants, Coca-Cola Distributors, and Ford dealers are backed by exclusive, proven franchise concepts, you will be backed with a charter membership in the most comprehensive mail-order program ever offered.

For more information, write to

Mail Order Associates
Dept. 101
120 Chestnut Ridge Road
Montvale, NJ   07645
(201) 391-3660

LADIES' AND CHILDREN'S CLOTHING /
Marlenna Fashions

The ladies' and children's clothing business is booming and Marlenna Fashions has available for you not one, but five, exciting retailing concepts to choose from if you want to capitalize on the profits you can now make (even spare-time) in the clothing business.

1. Ladies' Store

Since 1977, Marlenna Fashions has offered its Better Dress and Sportswear Store for the discriminating woman. With encouragement by Marlenna's tried and proven marketing concept, you may open and own one of the finest, if not the finest, fashion boutiques in your community. As you are probably well aware, many women hate to buy a garment if there are 12 or 15 of the exact same style hanging on the rack. Due to their "low minimum order" program, you can offer as many styles and brands as you so desire. Isn't it about time for a store in your community that offers fashion-conscious women a choice?

2. Children's Store

Marlenna Fashions also spans new horizons with the introduction of a successful children's program. As in the case of all apparel stores under the Marlenna Fashions name, the children's stores have access to the hottest-selling brands, with immediate delivery! How many children's stores in your community can boast that they carry 50 or more top brands under one roof? We bet only your store can make such a claim!

3. Off-Price Concept

A major trend in apparel retailing is the off-price concept. Simply put, this means selling first-quality, top-name merchandise at prices that are less than the normal retail price. An off-price store should not be confused with the typical discount store, which usually sells lower-end, discounted, or irregular merchandise. The off-price store offered by Marlenna Fashions sells nothing but the most current, first-quality merchandise available. We feel that an off-price store that offers top labels and great personal service can't help but be a winner.

4. Plus-Size Store

Over the past several years, Marlenna Fashions has been a leader in forecasting fashion trends. And currently, an emerging segment of the apparel industry is plus-size women's shops. Now, Marlenna Fashions has the resources for the best brand-name merchandise in the plus-size business.

The most exciting element of the plus-size business is the new updated styling available for the fashion-conscious woman. There was a time when all that was offered was polyester pull-on pants and coordinating tops for the plus-size customer. And in many towns, it's still the same! But now there are all the latest styles and fabrics for even the youngest, most fashion-conscious plus-sized customer!

Remember, Marlenna Fashions will be happy to assist you in merchandising your new store with either plus-size fashions or a combination of sizes, including juniors and misses.

5. $19.99 (and Less) Maximum Price Apparel Store

If you are interested in a high-volume, fast-paced retail business, Marlenna's Maximum Price Apparel Store may be just what you are looking for. In a maximum-price store, everything in your store will sell for a maximum price (for instance, $19.99) and less. When a customer comes into your store, there is no way to suffer from "sticker shock." The customer knows that *nothing* in your store is higher than that certain, specific price, and that many of the garments in your store will be selling for less than the maximum price. Word-of-mouth advertising by your customers will be your biggest asset.

You can open a Marlenna Fashions shop with minimum investment (depending on type of business, size, and location). Profits are exceptionally high because you buy right and have fast sales since you cater to one particular segment of the market. And, of course, Marlenna provides all the initial and ongoing training and support you need.

Any of these profitable merchandising concepts can be operated spare-time (or even absentee) and can be the beginning of an exciting career in fashion merchandising.

For more information, write to

Marlenna Fashions
2809 W. Fifteenth Street
Panama City, FL   32401
(904) 785-4111

MONOGRAMMING SERVICE / Meistergram

Solid support is one of the major benefits that Meistergram offers its licensees. Meistergram, a 56-year-old company that manufactures and distributes equipment and supplies for monogramming and embroidering on nearly everything from shirts to towels to tennis racket covers, is now on the fast track to growth. "We sell all the materials to help licensees start a monogramming business," says marketing services coordinator Mary K. Winstead. "Many people start successful businesses from their homes, both full- and part-time. Some gradually move into retail shops. It's amazing what an extremely viable business it is to operate out of the home. You can do it while raising a family. Sixty percent of our people have never done anything like this before," she adds.

Once you buy a Meistergram machine, you are trained at your own location. (Meistergram will travel anywhere in the world.) "And we don't just sell the machine," Winstead notes. "Once a machine is sold, [the buyer] is actively in the fold." Ongoing seminars and a newsletter inform operators about market trends, new technologies, and the type of work other people in the business are doing. Winstead adds that the home office is always available by phone to provide advice. "Just the other day, someone called to find out how to stitch on a bathing suit," she says.

Meistergrammers are constantly finding new applications for their craft. "It's limited only by the imagination," Winstead says. One man, for instance, set up shop on board a cruise ship, where he was kept busy personalizing more than enough items to pay for his trip. A South Carolina woman has been kept so busy monogramming corporate logos that she hasn't even hit the personal market she originally set out to target.

"We are always amazed at what people come up with," Winstead says. Many people are exploring applique work and other techniques to use with their machines. Meistergram sells many design packages such as borders, florals, and country patterns. And the company is constantly producing new cassettes for its equipment.

Monogramming has always been a part of finer fashions but it is becoming increasingly popular because fashions are becoming more personalized—and nothing can create more personalization than an individual's monogram. Monogramming is also a cost-effective way to create a quality image to clothing and accessories and an economical way for people to upgrade image without overspending on designer clothing.

With your monogramming equipment, you can provide direct service to consumers or rely primarily on retail accounts and tailoring and clothing shops for referral business. Most Meistergram dealers wisely go after both markets.

The machine and its accessories can run as high as $16,000–$20,000, a figure that Winstead admits might appear steep. But some people have made their investments back in as little as six months. Says Winstead, "If you're willing to work hard, the return is there."

For more information, write to

Meistergram
3517 W. Wendover Avenue
Greensboro, NC   27407
(800) 222-2600

MORTGAGE INTEREST REDUCING / Mortgage Reduction Consultants

California entrepreneur Russell Jones profitably spent the past three years teaching homeowners how to save money on their mortgage payments. And the money they save is astounding!

His company, Mortgage Reduction Consultants, specializes in showing homeowners how they can save $50,000 to $100,000 or more on their home mortgage without refinancing, points, qualifications, approvals, credit checks, or complicated paperwork. There is now a complete turnkey computer package available to others who want to become involved in the exciting and rewarding business of mortgage reduction services.

According to Jones, "Mortgage Reduction Consultants offers a complete business computer and Bi-Weekly Mortgage Reduction software designed to help homeowners save thousands on interest charges."

As a consultant you can pocket an average $500 consulting fee on every Bi-Weekly Mortgage Reduction program you set up for the millions of homeowners waiting to hear about the Bi-Weekly Mortgage Reduction plan.

Jones claims, "In any area there is probably only 1 in 500 homeowners that know anything about a Bi-Weekly Mortgage Plan. Yet a simple Video presentation will have them enrolling in a Preferred Bi-Weekly Plan that will put money in your pocket. They have everything to gain! Thus as a Mortgage Reduction Consultant, you become a valuable and welcomed resource."

USA Today has heralded the Bi-Weekly Mortgage Program as being "on its way to being the hottest home loan of the decade."

139

To understand the program, realize that in the United States we have the most expensive way to repay loans. No one in the world repays a loan in the ridiculous way we do. We pay interest in arrears, we pay interest on the unpaid balance, we compound the interest, and, on top of that, we amortize our loans for 30 years! If you have a $100,000 loan, you may repay $300,000 or more in payments before your loan is repaid.

The Canadians have a system that is incredibly less expensive compared to ours. There a borrower can take out the same $100,000 loan, with the same interest rate, and virtually the same monthly payments, but the loan will be repaid in 21 years instead of 30. An amazing $73,000 will have been saved in interest!

The reason for the tremendous difference is that Canadians repay their loans on a biweekly basis. Rather than making 12 monthly payments each year, as we do, they make a payment every two weeks. That's 26 payments each year, or the equivalent of 13 monthly payments. That thirteenth payment is what accounts for the huge savings in both time and interest.

Those same savings can be made on loans in this country through the use of a revolutionary program known as the "Preferred Bi-Weekly Mortgage System."

Mortgage Reduction Consultants offers a simple service: As a consultant, you find people with amortized loans, such as homeowners and commercial developers, and show them how to save thousands of dollars on interest charges by switching to a biweekly plan.

Why don't most people just switch over to biweekly mortgages themselves? According to Jones, there are very few banks that offer biweekly payment plans, and the homeowner who goes through conventional channels must pay expensive refinancing fees in order to originate a brand-new, biweekly loan.

To bypass this problem, Mortgage Reduction Consultants has a nondiscretionary trust service set up on a nationwide basis. This process allows a borrower to become a direct participating member in the "Preferred Bi-Weekly Mortgage Plan."

The complete Mortgage Reduction computer business package includes

1. A complete XT IBM-compatible computer system
2. A Preferred Bi-Weekly software package. This does not require any computer knowledge. Just a few figures, the push of a button, and you receive a complete printout.
3. A complete marketing system which includes ad slicks, flyers, direct mail pieces, and direct and phone presentations
4. Membership in the Bi-Weekly Association, which includes the benefit of hundreds of thousands of hours and dollars that have gone into its development
5. A video that explains the benefits of the Preferred Bi-Weekly Program
6. Personal guidance through Mortgage Reduction Consultants' professional consultants.

Now, you can become a mortgage reduction consultant and get in on the ground floor of a proven new way of helping people to save thousands of dollars on their existing mortgages.

Mortgage Reduction Consultants offers 100 percent financing, for those who qualify, for starting a mortgage reduction business. There is no special license required for starting this business. The only license that may be required is an occupational license.

For more information, write to

Mortgage Reduction Consultants
P.O. Box 910
El Dorado, CA   95623
(800) 876-6680

CREDIT REPAIR SERVICES / National Consumer Credit Foundation

Every day, thousands upon thousands of Americans are rejected for credit. Credit has become a big business, and people with poor credit pay large fees to have their credit restored so they can obtain bank credit cards, a car loan, or home mortgage, or perhaps even avoid bankruptcy.

Now you can get into the extremely lucrative credit repair business under a program established by the National Consumer Credit Foundation (NCCF). This nationwide organization is ready to train you as a credit counselor so you can help people permanently remove bankruptcies, repossessions, tax liens, judgments, and late payments from their credit record using little-known federal laws.

You can earn exceptional hourly income providing this valuable service. Clients pay $500 or more to repair credit, and the average case takes less than two hours to handle. You can earn even more if you choose to expand your service to debt consolidation and creditor workouts.

You can be fully trained and commissioned as a credit counselor for only $495. For this fee you receive a self-instructional ten-course program, telephone consultation, a full marketing program, and the official NCCF credit repair system (with all the forms and correspondence) that has proven so remarkably effective in solving credit problems for tens of thousands of grateful clients who deserved a chance for a better financial future.

Advertise for clients with small classified ads and wait for the fees to roll in. The NCCF marketing program guarantees you a continuous supply of clients all year long.

With this program, you receive an extensive assortment of professionally prepared, copyrighted advertisements, brochures, and sales aids that cost thousands of dollars to produce.

Service two or three clients a week (easily achieved on a Saturday) and earn $1,000–$1,500. Yes, the credit repair service is that profitable! All you need to get started is the training and support program that only the National Consumer Credit Foundation offers.

You can start doing business on a virtual shoestring and even work directly from your home.

There are more than 140 million Americans today who do not have a credit card. Other millions have urgent debt and credit problems that require immediate assistance. Your customers have problems to solve, and you will find they are highly motivated to retain your services. Your market potential is currently in the tens of millions—with new credit-impaired customers constantly being added.

Hundreds now make top money with their own credit repair service, and there's plenty of room for many more well-trained counselors.

For more information, write to

National Consumer Credit Foundation
366 SE Fifth Avenue
Delray Beach, FL   33483
(407) 243-3701

SHAVED-ICED CONFECTIONS / New Orleans Snowballs

If you've never tried it, you don't know what you're missing. There's nothing more delicious than an original New Orleans Snowball. Perhaps you didn't know you can make snowballs in New Orleans, but you can. You can also make New Orleans Snowballs in any other city or town—and make a small fortune in the process.

New Orleans Snowballs are a shaved-iced confection topped with fresh-made syrups to tempt any taste. Snowballs are the perfect thirst quencher. (Yes, people who try it really prefer it to ice cream by nearly two to one.) It is particularly popular with kids who love its distinctive flavor.

New Orleans Snowballs are based on a mom-and-pop small-business tradition of more than 50 years. So you have the secrets of a half-century of experience in producing a product that sells and sells and sells!

Set up a New Orleans Snowballs concession at a fair, flea market, or sporting or school event, or anywhere else you have throngs of people, and you'll have them standing in line. And the profits are fantastic. Your total cost (including container) is less than twelve percent, which gives you a far bigger profit margin than you can possibly earn with hum-drum ice cream. And once people sample their first New Orleans Snowball, you can bet they'll be back time and again for more.

You can even make delicious hot beverages with the New Orleans Snowball process. Snowballs are a winner in any climate or weather.

You can earn $300–$600 an hour for several hours' work on a weekend—making Snowballs a perfect spare-time opportunity. And it doesn't cost much to get started. For less than $6,000 you get all the equipment you need and a day and a half of training in the headquarters store. You'll learn both the secrets of "Snowballing" and how to run a profitable retail Snowball operation.

Snowballs can find a home any place there are crowds and other food concessions, because it's a one-of-a-kind item. This can be your chance to make money with a very different fast-food product with both wide market acceptance and no competition.

For more information, write to

New Orleans Snowballs
11 Carriage Square
Boone, NC   28607
(704) 262-3952

WINDSHIELD REPAIR /
Novus, Inc.

More than 8 million pitted car and truck windshields are replaced annually, at a cost of more than $2.4 billion. Up to 75 percent of these windshields could be repaired by Novus for one-fifth the cost of a new windshield. Novus' fast, inexpensive, permanent repair system predictably has attracted such huge fleet customers as Bell Telephone, General Mills, Eastman-Kodak, Bristol-Myers, Hertz, Avis, Budget, Federal Express, and many others that want to save big money on their windshield repairs.

Novus is an *international* franchise specializing in the repair of cracks, breaks, and scratches in vehicle windshields and commercial plate glass, so its reputation for excellence is well known. The company also manufactures and distributes proprietary polishes that clean, protect, and remove scratches and haze from most plastic surfaces, offering customers a full-service program.

Many Novus franchisees also repair plate glass in commercial buildings, retail stores, offices, factories, and warehouses, which significantly increases their income. Consequently, businesses avoid not only the higher cost of replacement, but also the expenses related to new signs, rewiring of alarm systems, and weatherstripping necessary when broken windows are replaced. In fact, major insurance companies are waiving the holder's deductible as an incentive for them to use the Novus windshield repair and thus avoid the higher cost of total windshield replacement.

Some 700 Novus franchisees and 1,500 dealers in more than 30 countries around the world reported sales of more than $30 million in 1988, making Novus *the* industry leader. The demand for this service will continue to be great.

Novus provides all the equipment and training you need to repair windshields professionally. Additionally, a dynamic marketing program is offered, which virtually guarantees instant profitability in this new and exciting industry.

There are tremendous profits to be made with the Novus system. You can repair about eight windshields a day and earn $400–$500. Land a fleet account and you can keep busy every day. But even without high-volume accounts, you can attract sufficient customers to bolster your income several hundred dollars a week. Work whatever hours you want. Marketing your services is easy. We know one Novus dealer who has local gas stations refer customers for a nominal referral fee, and this enterprising chap is making a fortune. Your investment is small, so Novus may be the perfect way to break into your own sideline business.

For more information, write to

Novus, Inc.
10425 Hampshire Avenue South
Minneapolis, MN   55438
(612) 944-8000
(800) 328-1117

ALL-OCCASION SIGNS / Outdoor Fun Signs

Things are getting a little weird in the neighborhood. Drive down Main Street and you'll notice signs curiously different from the "For Sale" announcements you usually spot. Heart-shaped signs bearing declarations of love, wedding bells proclaiming anniversary wishes, or blue or pink storks announcing new arrivals now adorn suburban lawns everywhere. Welcome to the newest genre of greeting cards—announcement signs!

Rather than send an ordinary card to show they care, people are opting instead for these large, eye-catching, sentimental expressions. Why spend time and money mailing birth announcements to your neighbors when you can proudly display on your lawn a stork sign disclosing all vital information about your newest family member? And instead of the unimaginative box of melted chocolates, or wilted roses, why not take a different, novel approach to sentimentality? You can, for example, plant a sign portraying a cuddly teddy bear with "I Love You" boldly embossed across his chest. The front yard of your betrothed can be the perfect place to express your affection.

In addition to graduations, weddings, or birthdays, people use these colorful announcement signs to welcome someone home, to announce a local high school reunion, to pronounce retirements, and for almost any other occasion. "Forty percent of the signs relate to birthdays, forty percent to storks (for birth announcements), fifteen percent for graduation announcements and the remaining five percent for miscellaneous occasions such as Just Married or Happy Anniversary," says Diane Shiffer, founder of Outdoor Fun Signs.

The idea for Outdoor Fun Signs first came to Shiffer when she was driving through her own neighborhood and saw a stork on someone's lawn. "That stork was from this guy who was just doing it part-time," she said. "I thought 'what a great idea!'" Shiffer thought the idea had enough potential to turn it into a thriving business. "Anything that people would buy flowers for, they'd rent a sign for," she observes. "Then I just started to think of all the other holidays, and the business was started."

Shiffer recently began to offer Outdoor Fun Signs as a franchise. A total franchise package costs $15,000 and includes 26 signs, plus all business and office supplies needed to run the business the first year. Territories are sold by county boundaries, so franchisees are limited to a particular county and are granted complete exclusivity.

Shiffer's franchise offer is detailed to the point of including even basic supplies such as file folders, gas mileage books, and mechanical pencils. She feels her company clearly stands out from the competition because she does more than provide signs, but also thoroughly equips each franchisee with every possible provision—ink markers, sales tax books, promotional flyers, 3×5 cards, business cards, colored paper—to show the detailed planning that guarantees the success of her program.

Profits from this business differ according to location and the income level of the people in the neighborhood. "I am in a relatively poor neighborhood," Shiffer says, "so people here aren't really willing to spend too much money on signs. But should you live where people are wealthier, you can charge more, and thereby make more."

Signs can rent for $10–$20 a day, so the return on investment per sign is tremendous. The only expense is advertising and delivery costs. Advertising can be a slight problem with this business, because there is no yellow page classification for this type of business. Moreover, most prospective customers don't know such a business even exists—and therefore are not likely to look for it.

Notwithstanding these problems, which many new businesses must overcome, Outdoor Fun Signs have high visibility, and the concept begins to spread rapidly through word of mouth.

American consumers are always on the lookout for new ways to send greetings—hence the singing telegram and the large, mylar balloons. It looks as though Diane Shiffer may have tapped into a new category in the novelty business. Her Outdoor Fun Signs are pointing confidently toward success!

For more information, write to

Outdoor Fun Signs
138 River Corner Road
Conestoga, PA   17516
(717) 872-6916
Contact: Diane Shiffer

BUILDING MAINTENANCE AND ROOFING / Pace Products

Pace specializes in building maintenance and roof-coating products. What makes Pace a salesperson's delight is that it exclusively features a Seamless Spray that has put Pace head and shoulders above the competition in the roof-coating business.

The market for this business is exceptional. Look around you at all of the buildings three years and older in your community. Every one is a prospect for Pace maintenance products. Your market consists of all commercial, institutional, and industrial buildings, so there is no limit to the number of good prospects. And that market is growing as the population and economy grows, adding virtually hundreds of prospects in even the smallest towns.

You decide your earnings with Pace. Seamless Spray sales automatically earn you $1,550 and more on a single order, and you can easily accomplish $25,000 to $30,000 in annual earnings on a part-time basis—even more if you devote 40 hours a week to Pace, which many reps who began part-time now do.

No skill or extensive training is required to become an independent Pace distributor. You receive your self-contained Pace kit with full instructions and continuous help from your contact person at Pace Products, Inc.

The people Pace selects to sell its exclusive line of products are a special group, indeed. To Pace it is very important that they identify with the very best products of their kind and with a company that enjoys worldwide fame and recognition. They like being their own boss, setting their own hours, deciding how large their income should be, and being part of the finest sales force in the building maintenance industry.

As a Pace distributor, you're in business for yourself. You work for yourself, with no one to tell you what to do.

Pace has a proven record in the roof-repair business. Its unique spray is exceptionally easy to apply and is economical, and because it is a seamless application there are no problems with leaks. And Pace roof repairs last as long as—or longer than—any other roof-repair system on the market, giving your customers very good value for the money. Pace has an outstanding name and reputation in the maintenance products field, and a name your customers can accept with complete confidence. This makes it very easy to sell Pace Seamless Spray to the tens of thousands of property owners with roofing problems.

This opportunity can be yours with absolutely no investment now or in the future!

For more information, write to

Pace Products, Inc.
Dept. BK
Box 10925
11775 West 112th Street
Overland Park, KS   66210
(913) 469-5588

PACKAGING AND MAILING SERVICE /
Pack 'N' Mail
Mailing Center

Fifteen million plus—that is how many packages are sent daily through the UPS and U.S. mail systems, and this figure dramatically increases each year. Wouldn't you like to be a part of this growing industry?

Most individuals who wrestle with the occasional packaging of an item readied for shipment experience intimidation, frustration, and a tinge of fear that the parcel will never reach its destination. And they are often right. But wherever a solution is needed, some bright-eyed entrepreneur is more than willing to provide the answer.

Mike Gallagher of Lubbock, Texas not only thought there should be a better way for mailing packages, but his lifelong, consuming interest in business seized the moment.

He launched Pack 'N' Mail in 1981 in Hobbs, New Mexico, and then moved to Lubbock in 1985. He now operates three stores, which provide everything from packaging to recommendations of transportation. Gallagher says the service is one of the hottest growth industries existing today. It's a new concept. Every day you meet new people, get to know your regular customers, and solve the problem of customer deadlines.

"We have eliminated the hassle in the shipping business," he claims. Gallagher uses all available shippers in his packaging and mailing service. "I can give you a rate from everyone; tomorrow, second day or slow boat to China. You can pick the company you want to deal with, the rate you want to pay and the time of destination.

"When I started this business, it was my actual dream to be doing what I am doing right now," he says, referring to the opening of a chain of stores. Gallagher has helped in opening 115 stores that bear the Pack 'N' Mail name, but he has no continuing royalty or financial interest in any of them. His remuneration for assisting the independently owned businesses is a one-time consulting fee.

"I have no control over them at all," he says of the stores opened by other owners. "But I will help them throughout their first few months. I will help five years, if they need help." His rationale for continuing support for the stores is to make them successful so that he can continue opening stores on the consulting-fee basis. However, he expects to franchise his opportunity soon. Under that basis, he expects to charge a royalty fee of about 4 percent.

"First we screen our people. It's not enough just to have the money. If we open a lot of stores and half go out of business, that's not good." Gallagher has namesake stores scheduled to open soon in Peoria, Illinois; Lancaster, California; Virginia Beach, Virginia; and Hawaii.

With a good advertising and marketing plan, stores can expect to gross more than $200,000 in their first year. In fact, most stores will increase daily business 29 percent after their first month in business. Low start-up costs, low overhead, and a small staff make it possible for an excellent return on investment.

"I have been in this business since 1981, but started selling other stores two and a half years ago. We have sold over 115 stores in this short time, selling stores on an average of one per week," says Gallagher.

The most important part of Pack 'N' Mail is that the consulting fee is only $17,500, which is less than most franchise fees. There are no royalties to be paid—ever. This is a one-time fee. A full-line store costs $30,000–$35,000 for everything, from Gallagher's consulting fee to the up-front money for a building lease, and even down to the trash cans and ink pens. A small operation can be started for as little as $20,000.

Pack 'N' Mail is also an excellent spare-time opportunity because it's easy to recruit and train employees to staff the operation, so it naturally lends itself to absentee ownership.

There are a number of recent franchise entrants in the packaging and shipment business, but Pack 'N' Mail remains one of the best because Mike spends so much time training his clients and watching over their progress until he is confident they will succeed. As with so many businesses, support and supervision can be the difference between success and failure, and you won't find better support than with Mike Gallagher and Pack 'N' Mail Mailing Center.

For more information, write to

**Pack 'N' Mail Mailing Center
5701 Slide Road, Suite C-100
Lubbock, TX   79414
(806) 797-3400
(800) 759-2424, Ext. 444**

FACSIMILE NAME-BRAND FRAGRANCES /
Paris Perfumes

If you think it's Poison perfume but it's not, it could be part of a sweet-selling wave in the fragrance industry: designer knock-off perfumes. From Joy to Obsession, nearly every desirable designer scent is now available in duplicate at an average savings of 80 percent. These great impostors are becoming so popular that the annual market for knock-off fragrances has grown from virtual insignificance to $450 million since 1980.

Apparently, as the perfume-cloning industry gets older, it gets better. Though the cheap, watered-down imitations of yore may still exist, the biggest growth in this segment has come in the form of fine fragrances that claim to be indistinguishable from costly originals, in terms of either scent or quality.

Perfume manufacturers create duplicate formulas through some fairly sophisticated techniques. Patent conflicts are generally not a problem, since most perfume formulas are not patented. (Such information becomes public knowledge.) Advanced technology now makes it possible to determine the various components of a fragrance. Armed with this information, master perfumers then work to achieve the right balance of ingredients. All in all, it takes a fair amount of equipment and expertise to make an acceptable clone, but some companies do it exceptionally well.

Paris Perfumes is a world-leading seller of cloned perfumes. Its French perfumers have captured the aromas of the originals with such skill, we challenge you to tell the difference. In fact, they are so sure that you won't be able to tell the difference, they'll send you samples of their versions of Giorgio, Chanel No.

5, Joy, Opium, and Shalimar perfumes absolutely free. Now that's a challenge!

Now you can discover how easy it is to make money by becoming a Paris Perfume dealer selling these low-cost versions of the world's most expensive perfumes. You can offer your customers tremendous savings from the originals when you become a Paris Perfume dealer. For example, the original best-selling perfume from Beverly Hills—Giorgio—sells for $150 per ounce. Paris Perfume's version of Giorgio can be sold to your customers for only $15—that's 90 percent off the original price—and you pay only $5 and keep $10 for each and every bottle you sell. If your customer orders $60 worth of perfumes, at 90 percent off the original prices you keep $40, and so on. That's 200 percent profit on each and every order you write. Once your customers have the opportunity to smell these versions of the originals, you'll be writing up orders as fast as you can, and because of their high quality, repeat orders will be effortless.

This is one great line to sell through party plans. What we particularly like about Paris Perfumes is that it can be featured with other related product lines such as cosmetics, artificial gemstones, and jewelry—and even lingerie. This can be an ideal opportunity if you already sell one or more of these lines, because they are natural "tie-ins" creating plus sales.

You can easily earn several hundred dollars a week selling Paris Perfumes—and much more with an active party plan program. Competition is virtually nonexistent. (You can only find clones in a few exclusive shopping malls.) With Paris Perfumes you'll have the confidence of knowing you have the best clone line on the market today, and your many customers will appreciate the fact that they can enjoy the scents of some of the world's finest fragrances for a small fraction of the price they once paid for the original.

For more information, write to

Paris Perfumes
768 Carver Avenue
Westwood, NJ   07675
(201) 387-7909

COLOR FILM PROCESSING PROMOTION / Phototron Express

Everyone seems to be a photo buff nowadays, and Phototron has turned this fact into what might be the hottest spare-time money-making concept this year.

Phototron sells an attractive, wallet-sized Gold Card redeemable for 200 rolls of nationally advertised color print film —in any size or exposure—exclusively to its marketing representatives from coast to coast. Gold Cards cost Phototron representatives only $3 each. It sounds incredible, but it's true! The recommended selling price is $20. Needless to say, Gold Cards sell very well. But what really thrills Gold Card customers most is the company's low developing costs which rival the price of any drugstore, Fotomat, or mail-away program.

Phototron recommends placing the Gold Cards in beauty parlors, allowing beauticians to sell them to their customers for $20 each. Customers love to buy the Gold Cards because of their excellent value, and for very little effort the beauty parlor receives $5 per sale. Since Phototron representatives pay only $3 apiece, they would earn a net profit of $12 per sale. What's really exciting is that each beauty parlor sells, on average, between 10 and 20 Gold Cards each week! And Phototron representatives have a wide roster of beauty parlors selling the Gold Cards, so the profits pour in.

The minimum order is 50 Gold Cards at $3 each. Included with the initial order are compelling sales posters for the beauty parlors and, of course, the Marketing Report, which gives you tons of inside information on how to make money with Gold Cards. On your first order, should you order 100 Gold Cards instead of 50, Phototron sends you an additional 50 Gold Cards at no additional cost. This is their way of helping new representatives get off to a very profitable start with the company, because the rep would now earn $150 additional income.

Phototron thoroughly guides its representatives through successful salesmanship techniques. The company provides fund-raising and telephone scripts that get excellent sales results, furnishes an ad slick for mail orders, and offers unique tips for introducing the Gold Cards in beauty parlors and other outstanding retail outlets.

Another successful marketing method Phototron recommends is to sell Gold Cards by phone and tip the telemarketing salesperson $5 per sale. The average telephone salesperson can take orders for 4–8 Gold Cards per hour, so income can be attractive to even the most talented telemarketer.

This is the perfect sideline business because there are almost no start-up costs, you set your own hours, and you can work directly from your home. The Phototron program has been running for several years, so it's not a short-term venture but one with long-term potential.

To maximize profits for each representative, the number of representatives in each geographical area is limited. To find out if there is an opening in your area, call today. If none is available, your name will be put on a waiting list.

The earnings potential with Gold Cards is unlimited. Once the Gold Cards are placed in beauty parlors they sell themselves, so your job is basically to keep each location restocked, collect your $12 profit on each Gold Card sold, and spend your spare time scouting additional beauty parlors as Gold Card outlets. Of course, Gold Cards can be sold in locations other than beauty parlors, but most reps sell so many cards through beauty parlors that they seldom need to seek other types of outlets.

Phototron doesn't plan to distribute Gold Cards other than through its exclusive reps, so you have no competition. For each Gold Card sold within your territory, you *must* earn a profit. Maybe that's why Phototron's reps say selling Gold Cards is like having your own exclusive gold mine.

For more information, write to

Phototron Express, Inc.
4321 W. College Avenue
Appleton, WI   54914
(800) 426-5266

PICTURE BUSINESS CARDS / Positive Concepts, Ltd.

Business cards are no longer just a way of providing names and telephone numbers. It is a visualization of what is offered, or the people who offer it.

The Trump Card is so much more than a business card. The Trump Card is an actual photograph on Kodak paper, and like other photographs, it is not thrown away as are ordinary business cards. Even if the printed business card is kept long enough to be filed, people usually can't remember who gave it to them. Not only is the Trump Card kept, but there is an instant recall of that person. Most people agree they can remember faces better than names. The Trump Card gives you both.

Trump Cards are so unique and different that they become a conversation piece, which promotes word-of-mouth and referral business time and time again.

The Trump Card is one of the most exciting, well-received, low-cost marketing and advertising tools ever introduced, and it can work wonders for your customers no matter what type of business they are in.

Positive Concepts, Ltd. is an Atlanta-based corporation that has successfully been in the picture business-card business since 1982. The success of its distributors is positive proof of its unprecedented marketing and training program. Articles about the company, its product, and its distributors have been printed throughout the country both in newspapers and in national publications.

There is money to be made with Trump Cards. With hustle you can easily make $300–$500 a week part-time, because markups are so extraordinarily high.

Sales are steady because most of your business will come

from repeat orders. Once you sell a customer you can earn money year after year, as picture business cards are rapidly distributed.

As part of the Positive Concepts program, you are provided leads of prospective customers who respond to Positive Concepts' nationwide advertising. Positive Concepts does much more for you in making your business a huge success. You are given all the marketing tools you could possibly need to aggressively sell your service on your own.

You'll also receive complete training covering all aspects of owning and operating a business, including sales and photography. But don't think you have to have experience as a photographer to qualify for this opportunity. The photographic skills required are minimal (if you can take a picture with an ordinary camera, you have what it takes), and what little you must know Positive Concepts teaches you.

Working with Positive Concepts, you can produce the finest photo business cards on the market, because the company has the technology and experience to show you how to produce attractive cards each and every time.

What will this opportunity cost? Only $6,000 secured by sales aids and equipment. This can be a very *small* investment for a very *big* future!

For more information, write to

Positive Concepts, Ltd.
561 Thornton Road
Lithia Springs, GA   30057
(404) 941-7940

EXECUTIVE PRODUCTIVITY TRAINING |
Priority Management Systems, Inc.

Executive and employee productivity has become a major concern for every size and type of business.

Priority Management Systems, Inc. (PM), an international management-training franchisor, trains its franchisees to work with individuals (primarily business executives) to be more effective and productive in their jobs. This is accomplished through intensive hands-on workshops with follow-up one-on-one consultations to fine-tune workshop training. Priority Management has thus far trained more than 200,000 individuals from more than 30,000 companies, making PM an industry leader. The training program's success rate is over 90 percent, much to the delight of PM's many clients.

To handle growing demand, there are now nearly 200 franchises in Canada, the United States, Australia, Great Britain, and New Zealand. The company sold 52 franchises in 1988 alone and projects nearly 100 new franchisees coming on board each year. Twelve percent of new franchise sales are to existing PM franchisees, validating franchise satisfaction with the program.

The primary market for Priority Management is the training of middle and upper management executives from small to Fortune 500 firms. Franchisees also train people in government and service organizations, so they really reach an unlimited market with their highly effective—and profitable—service.

The franchise fee is $27,500, with a 9 percent royalty and a 1 percent annual advertising fee. It takes an investment of about $35,000–$45,000 to start a PM franchise, so it's a franchise for sideliners serious about what they do.

Although the concept suggests you should be a management guru, the reality is that no prior management training experience is necessary. The company whips franchisees into shape with a one-week intensive training program covering every aspect of operating the business. Ongoing training is through periodic updates, in-person visits by corporate personnel, and informative newsletters.

PM effectiveness training works in three distinct phases. Phase one is a four-and-a-half-hour workshop. Phase two, 10-14 days later, is a 15-minute to one hour one-on-one session to fine-tune what was learned at the workshop. Phase three, two weeks later, is a three-and-a-half-hour workshop to reinforce the first workshop and the personal session.

If you like to interact with others and have good organizational and teaching skills, this can be just what you are looking for. And you can choose your hours, making it an ideal spare-time business opportunity.

The key to success in this business is the ability, willingness, and hustle to sell productivity training to new accounts. Virtually every company is a candidate, but few recognize their need for increased productivity.

If you think you have what it takes to sell—and deliver—a service that can substantially improve productivity and profits for your clients, then Priority Management Systems wants to talk to *you.*

For more information, write to

Priority Management Systems, Inc.
2401 Gateway Drive, Suite 115
Irving, TX   75063
(214) 550-1981

SOFT TUBS / PRO C.I.R. Property Improvements, Ltd.

According to the U.S. Consumer Products Safety Commission, there are more than 150,000 bathtub-related hospital emergencies each year. People usually slip on the wet surface or fall and hurt themselves by striking the hard edges of the traditional porcelain tub.

Alarmed by the growing number of injuries to older citizens, the American Association of Retired Persons (AARP) is currently lobbying Congress to have a bill passed that it be mandatory that any federal- or state-funded project for the disabled and retired have a "soft-cushioned" bathtub. The trend toward soft-cushioned bathtubs is growing on its own as many developers, nursing home owners, and senior citizen facilities are discovering the safety of these tubs in contrast to the conventional tubs.

Enter PRO C.I.R. Property Improvements Ltd., a Vancouver, British Columbia firm that is revolutionizing the tub industry with its new soft tub.

This pioneering Canadian firm has a complete line of tubs ranging from basic to high-tech tubs with fiber optic lighting designs and hydrojets to meet any decor or lifestyle need. These tubs are not only attractive and versatile, but the closest you can come to accidentproof.

PRO C.I.R. is currently rounding up potential distributors who want to cash in on the soft tubs market. A distributorship sells for about $10,000 per 1 million in population. According to PRO's Greg Forrest, "Good candidates are individuals with some building or home improvement experience, so that they are capable of installing the tubs themselves."

PRO C.I.R. was selected as one of the *100 Best* because we

believe its product has enormous sales potential, particularly if legislation requiring soft tub installation is enacted.

But even without such laws, there will be millions of people who prefer soft tubs to the more dangerous, conventional tub. This certainly will be true of older people, who account for an increasing percentage of the population.

This can be an exceptionally profitable sideline business because there is absolutely no competition, and soft tubs is not a price-sensitive item. Moreover, you have an easily reached market focusing on older and disabled people.

Soft tubs can be an excellent additional line if you are in the plumbing or home improvement business, or offer related products to the senior citizen market. Profits per sale can be exceptionally high (depending on the style and number of tubs sold). Marketing soft tubs is easily accomplished, as the company makes available a complete marketing program that has already proven enormously successful in several test markets.

This is one opportunity to keep a close eye on (or better still, to act on) before the best territories are grabbed by other opportunity seekers.

For more information, write to

PRO C.I.R. Property Improvements Ltd.
Vancouver, British Columbia
Canada   V6G 1P6
(604) 688-7711

DISC JOCKEY ENTERTAINMENT / The Pro's

They may not sing tunes or play instruments, but The Pro's consider themselves musical entertainers nonetheless.

The Pro's are the mobile disc jockeys of Sound Entertainment, a fast-growing Philadelphia-based firm that specializes in providing recorded music for parties and special occasions and otherwise turning such events into fun-packed gala festivities not to be soon forgotten.

Under the Pro banner, some 100 DJs spend their time hopping from anniversary to birthday party, bar mitzvah to wedding. Their job is not only to spin records, but to become the nucleus of the festivity—pleasing the crowd, leading musical games, and keeping the party going with plenty of fun and frivolity.

"This is a people business," Pro's training director Mike Brandt recently warned a class of DJ trainees. "You're an entertainer. It's your moral obligation to give the people the best show you can." And they do. Thousands of times a year!

Sound Entertainment is the brainchild of Herb Cohen. In 1977, he began spinning discs at bar and bas mitzvahs. He was 17 and already knew his life's ambition. "It was great for my ego," Cohen says. He then started doing parties for the parents of these teenagers. And they were fabulous successes.

Before long, Cohen was receiving more than one job offer a night. "I just couldn't be in two places at once," he says.

So a business is born!

"I thought the idea of a disc-jockey service was a fantastic opportunity," he says. "It was economically feasible because hiring a DJ is cheaper than hiring a band, and we could offer a variety of music—from big band to top 40."

Today, a staff of 20 Pro supervisors oversees some 100 DJs—the largest such operation in the area.

Since most DJs work on a part-time basis, disc jockeying attracts a wide assortment of people—from accountants to salespeople, homemakers to horse groomers. Becoming a DJ can be fun for anyone who enjoys music and parties.

Each year, The Pro's do some 10,000 parties throughout New Jersey, Pennsylvania, Delaware, and Maryland, according to Cohen. Additionally, some DJs hold once-a-week gigs at area nightclubs.

Local DJs join The Pro's as trainees. Although trainees do not get paid, the instruction program is free, and Sound Entertainment picks up travel expenses to these parties.

Once training is successfully completed, each DJ is given record equipment; a set of lights including a strobe, mirror ball, flood, and colored mood lights; and a case of 800 45s before each show.

Each DJ receives a base salary, Cohen says, and is permitted to pocket all tips, as well as beforetime and overtime money that is earned beyond the standard four-to-five-hour affair.

But this can turn into serious money for 4–5 hours' work. Some Pro DJs report that they can go home with $500 for a night's work if the host thinks the DJ did a good job and shows appreciation with a hefty tip.

In addition, a DJ gets paid a certain fee for referrals—each time someone hires The Pro's and mentions the DJ's name. So, if you live within The Pro's market area—and enjoy entertaining—you have a great opportunity to have a good time while earning spare-time income.

The Pro's are now franchising their concept throughout the United States. Terms and fees vary depending on the area and amount of support required. They are even exploring joint ventures with other entrepreneurs in the entertainment-related field.

The Pro's offer a proven concept. They have both the name and the experience to get you into the entertainment business—with virtually no investment on your part. This is one opportunity you won't want to pass up if you think you'd like to turn music into money.

For more information, write to

**The Pro's
9045 Ashton Drive
Philadelphia, PA   19136
(215) 843-7667
(800) 843-7667**

DIRECT-RESPONSE PRODUCT FINDERS / Quantum Marketing International, Inc.

Ginsu Knives, Closet Space Savers, The Fabulous Mouli-M2 French Processor. These are products successfully sold by the tens of thousands every day on cable TV.

Direct-response advertising has evolved so rapidly, the industry cannot even measure the enormous quantity of products sold through TV. But two things are for certain—TV marketing is quickly catching up with conventional retailing as a way to bring new products to the attention of consumers, and *hot* products do sell like wildfire with the right TV promotion.

That's where you come in.

TV marketing firms are *hungry* for new and exciting products but have neither the time nor the resources to find all the products they could market successfully. So they need part-timers to locate novel and new products for the TV market (or that will sell well with print advertising).

Quantum Marketing International, Inc., a leader in TV product marketing, can put you in your own spare-time product-finder business as a scout for products it can sell. You invest nothing but some time and the ability to stay alert for products you think can become best-sellers on TV. Quantum does the rest. You then simply sit back and earn a hefty commission on every item sold. A good product, according to Quantum's Vice-President, Tim Harrington, can produce six-figure commissions, so the prospective rewards are better than good—they are enormous!

Quantum's general approach is to develop a private-label product with a manufacturer and either foot the whole bill for the project or joint-venture product promotion with the manufacturer. Among its nationally known programs are Arnold's Gourmet Kitchen (which sells "The Blade", a 20-piece knife and garnishing set for $39.95); The Fabulous Wok of China, another $39.95 winner; and its latest, The Mouli-M2, a French food processor selling in droves for $29.95.

Harrington reports projects on the drawing board for unique steam irons and other exciting novel home products. To boost sales even more, big-name celebrities soon may host future programs. Certain types of programs don't spell success, he advises: those selling "prevention," such as anti-theft alarms, water purifiers, and radon-detection kits. He reports being approached by a number of companies on the latter, "but we've stayed away from it because we'd be selling negativity. People don't see an immediate benefit in products like this."

Where can you find new products to generate those big commission checks for you? Flea markets, crafts studios, from inventors, overseas bazaars—these are just a few of the thousands of places where tomorrow's best-sellers may be lurking today. Maybe you already have that hot product in mind. Quantum is equally interested in home-study courses, educational material, and unique new services that lend themselves to TV direct marketing. For example, Quantum markets Ed Beckley's course on "How To Buy Real Estate With No Cash Down," and it has become one of the most successful lines. There are plenty of other home-study courses that have huge sales potential, Harrington reminds us.

Why not get in touch with the folks at Quantum? It costs you absolutely nothing to find out whether your product has what it takes to produce those big commission checks.

Quantum would be pleased to send you more information about the company, the type of products it is looking for, and how you can earn big money—spare-time—as a sleuth in Quantum's new product squad!

For more information, write to

Quantum Marketing International, Inc.
550 Time Town Road, Suite 350
Fort Washington, PA   19034
(215) 283-0871
Contact: Tim Harrington

MATERIAL AND GLASS REPAIR / Repair-It

Repair-It is *the* opportunity for making money in your own sideline business repairing vinyl, leather, glass, fabric, velour, and formica. Operate this business right from your own home, in your own hours, with little overhead, and pocket 90 cents out of every dollar as pure profit.

Customers are so abundant that it's hard not to find them in every building on every block on the street. Restaurants, hotels, car dealers, motels, churches, hospitals, beauty shops, buses, schools, theaters, body shops, airplanes, and most of all average homeowners all need Repair-It. Not only do these customers have damaged vinyl, leather, glass, and fabrics—but very often these damages occur on a weekly basis, guaranteeing you repeat business.

It is quite surprising to find out how many thousands of people do repair work and make big money with it. Donna Purpura, working the Chicago area, grossed more than $100,000 in 1988 with Repair-It, and we have spoken to many, many other craftspeople who have made more than $50,000 per year. You too can make a substantial amount of money with the Repair-It program. And you can start part-time and work it into a full-time business once you see how profitable it can be!

The Repair-It program utilizes special processes invented and patented by Larry Speer, the Repair-It founder. His unique process for fabric repair is the only one in this country approved by GM and Chrysler, so we feel it must do a first-class job.

Repair-It is really four business opportunities for the price of one, because you can repair not only vinyl and leather, but windshield glass, fabric and velour, and even formica counter-tops as well. And this powerful money-making opportunity can be yours for less than $1,000 (and as little as $100 if you want only the vinyl and leather kit).

Repair-It furnishes complete dealer training with optional training programs at its Ohio plant, or you may elect a convenient home-study program. Repair-It also helps you promote your service locally on cable TV with its exclusive TV commercial ready for presentation in your local area. No other business opportunity in America today in vinyl, leather, glass, or formica repair has this TV program, or the ability to land you so many happy customers.

Profits are tremendous in this business. Ten dollars of repair compound can often earn you in excess of $200 profit. If you are willing to work with your hands and are willing to put in a few hours every day on a no-nonsense program, you can earn an exceptional livelihood with Repair-It.

Start part-time (operate out of your own home) and watch the profits build up. You can easily expand by adding employees to keep up with the growing volume. We know of Repair-It dealers raking it in with as many as 10–12 employees constantly on the road servicing clients.

Contact Repair-It. Once you see how easily and professionally Repair-It solves fabric defects, you'll be as convinced as we are that Repair-It can be one hot opportunity!

For more information, write to

Repair-It Industries, Inc.
440 W. Hopocan Avenue
Barberton, OH   44203
(216) 745-0069
Contact: Lawrence L. Speer, President

ROBOTIC BOXING PROMOTIONS / Rocky-Bots

Today's sports-minded entrepreneurs are earning megabuck incomes hosting robotic boxing tournaments in local bars, clubs, restaurants, town fairs, and festivals and even at corporate-sponsored events where "Rocky-Bots" are the latest rage.

"Rocky-Bots" are two four-foot-tall robots that cleverly box in a 4' × 6' ring. Their punches are guided by customers who are eager to pay entry fees of about $2 to $5 each for the excitement of trading jabs, hooks, and uppercuts with an opponent who coughed up his own fee.

The completely portable boxing robots and ring setup allow entrepreneurs to earn a part-time income on the average of $30,000 to $60,000 a year, which is more than many real-life boxing promoters earn.

Rocky-Bots are the invention and brainchild of former arm wrestling and dart tournament promoter Keith Namanny of Cumberland, Iowa. This entrepreneurial sports fanatic came up with the idea for robot boxing "out of desperation"; he says, "I was getting tired of thinking about having to take a 9-to-5 job. I decided to develop a fun item for sports enthusiasts.

"With the growing audience of wrestling and boxing fans across the U.S., it seemed logical to develop a fun participatory sport for these dedicated fans," says Namanny.

"I invested $1,200 into developing working models of the robots. A local blacksmith welded the framework together and I springloaded the arms for clean punching, and added lights and buzzers to make the boxing more exciting," boasts Namanny. Namanny "dressed" the robots with wigs, costumes and jewelry to closely resemble "Rocky" and "Mr. T."

174

Namanny quickly booked the Rocky-Bots at fairs, town festivals, bars, nightclubs, and mall and corporate promotions. "I charged organizations anywhere from $250 to $500 to rent the robots for a function as a promotional draw. I also make money charging tournament players a few dollars to box," he says.

"The crowd—young, old, male, female—really goes wild. I quickly started to receive calls from people across the country who wanted to get into robotic boxing and offer their own Rocky-Bots tournaments in their areas," says Namanny.

Namanny now charges individuals $5,000 to purchase their own two robots and ring.

"I have people who write and tell me that by sponsoring two tournaments a week, they are making a part-time income of $30,000 a year. Based on a per-tournament booking fee of $250, individuals who run 4 tournaments a week can make $60,000 a year," says Namanny.

"I suggest promoters charge $250 a tournament to be competitive with what local rock or country western bands charge per gig as they are often the competition for the Rocky-Bots.

"I do have one Rocky-Bots boxing operator in Rochester who charges $500 per tournament and makes a nice six-figure income each year from Rocky-Bots," says Namanny.

The $5,000 fee for the Rocky-Bots and ring also includes a two-day training seminar, a referee shirt and bell, posters, newsletters, sales assistance, a video, and tips on how to attract big-name corporate sponsors. (Both Coors and Genesee Brewing Company have been involved with big-revenue-generating sponsorships.)

Namanny charges an additional $495 annual fee to renew the robotic boxing license. The "dues" money is put toward producing the newsletter and distributing additional sales aids.

"The only things I don't include in the $5,000 purchase price are the optional items: white tuxedo, public address system and a weigh-in scale," says Namanny.

The sports entrepreneur has done so well in his few-year Rocky-Bots venture that he's hired a staff of four to help him assemble and ship the robots and process requests for his newly formed World Robotic Boxing Association.

But how do you make money being a "Rocky-Bot" promoter, you ask? Several ways. First of all, from the bar owners who pay you a booking fee of $250 to have you come in and conduct the event; and secondly, from the contestants who pay a $3 entry fee to enter the tournament, and you usually average 30 or more contestants per tournament. So you can bring in between $300 and $400 a night including sponsorship fees and T-shirt and cap sales. Not too shoddy for three to four hours' worth of fun.

Bar owners love the action and continue to rebook because Rocky-Bots is something new and different. It draws good crowds and brings new people into their bar every time. As more and more managers bring their stables of boxers to the tournaments around the circuit, its popularity increases. Priced right (usually the same as or often less than a band)—the bottom line as far as the bar owner and beer sponsor is concerned—Rocky-Bots increases product sales. When there is a band, everybody is dancing. With Rocky-Bots, only two people are; everybody else is drinking. In addition, it's a sport that they can see growing right in their own bar every time they book you. It's a great way for them to build a new clientele.

Rocky-Bots recently won first place in the sports and recreation division and second place "The Best of Show" at a four-state regional inventors' fair. The sport has really taken off since it did so well at the inventors' fair. Because it is so different, Rocky-Bots receives a lot of free publicity on TV and in the newspapers and generates a lot of interest.

If you ever wanted to own your own sport, the Rocky-Bots may be just the ticket you've been looking for. The total investment to become a Rocky-Bots promoter is only $3,600, which includes an exclusive territory, complete training on how to set up your sports-promotion business, and everything else you need to get going, making this a complete turnkey program.

You can start promoting on a part-time basis and work into a full-time venture as your account list grows.

Why not become a promoter of your own Rocky-Bots? It can be a fun (and profitable) way to wile away your spare-time hours.

For more information, write to

The World Robotic Boxing Association
183 N. Main Street
Cumberland, IA   50843
(712) 774-2577

BASEMENT DEWATERING AND RADON PREVENTION / Safe-Aire, Inc.

Basement water seepage is a problem wherever there are basements and sufficient rainfall or a high water table. Radon, another homeowner problem, has been found in every area of the country, and concern over this harmful gas is just beginning. Under state and federal laws, homeowners will be required to mitigate their homes of Radon prior to any sales transaction if Radon levels are unacceptable. In fact, EPA estimates project the radon-alleviation industry to be twice the size of asbestos abatement. This means there is a huge market of tens of thousands of homes with either water seepage or radon problems waiting for an effective and efficient system for alleviating these pesky and dangerous problems.

Basement De-Watering/Safe-Aire is the nation's largest dealer network of professional basement dewatering and radon-mitigation contractors. Established in 1978, BDW/SA dealers presently have exclusive rights to install the only patented radon-mitigation system in the nation. This is an EPA-proven method, which is capable of reducing harmful radon gases up to 99 + percent, as well as eliminating any water-seepage problems a property owner may have.

Experts consider BDW/SA system applications to be the most cost-effective and overall efficient methods on the market today for radon or water problems. Ease of installation (usually one working day), minimal fixed overhead, well-above-average profit margins—combined with a proven marketing approach to target clientele—provide dealers with unlimited sales potential and profit opportunity. Dealers' return on initial investment can easily and quickly be recovered within 90 days. BDW/SA dealers are also the nationally recognized basement environmental experts in water control and radon mitigation, and this means market acceptance by troubled homeowners.

BDW/SA dealers are thoroughly trained on method application, products, organizational start-up, and marketing as well as provided continuous dealer support programs held at national headquarters. Skills needed for operation are systematically provided to ensure the dealers ongoing success.

In addition to these benefits, some of the other less obvious but no less valuable advantages of affiliation with Basement Dewatering include

- Sales, marketing, and installation advice and troubleshooting assistance available through a toll-free 800 number
- Letters of introduction to local newspapers, realtors, and so forth
- News releases when you open or expand your business
- Inclusion on the HUD bidders' list. Safe-Aire the only national company listed under both "Waterproofing" and "Radon Mitigation."

Your total investment to become a BDW/SA dealer is only $14,500. This not only gives you the initial inventory and training, but guarantees you'll be the only authorized dealer per 300,000 population.

Many dealerships start out as spare-time businesses and because of BDW/SA's profitability quickly become full-time endeavors.

Basement dewatering and radon prevention are basically a service business, so it even can be operated from your home with little or no overhead. This industry claims to have one of the highest profit margins. You can earn $500–$1,000 a day as a Safe-Aire dealer and you can work the hours you choose. Many Safe-Aire dealers work only one or two evenings a week on sales calls and perform the work on Saturdays—and gross $30,000–$50,000 a year.

The strength of this business is that it is recession-proof. People need this service in good times and bad. Moreover, you have no direct competition because no competitive system can claim to have Safe-Aire's outstanding track record in water elimination or radon prevention. You can be proud to represent the Safe-Aire name.

For more information, write to

Safe-Aire, Inc.
162 E. Chestnut Street
Canton, IL   61520
(309) 647-0331
(800) 331-2943
Contact: Bill Wherley

HEAVY-DUTY CLEANING SERVICES / Servpro Industries, Inc.

Since 1967, Servpro Industries, Inc. has been growing into one of the giants of the franchised cleaning industry through a combination of careful diversification within the cleaning field and superior franchisee support.

Servpro was started when Ted Isaacson broke away from another cleaning firm where he was the largest franchisee; he had decided to start his own company to offer a new concept in cleaning.

One feature Isaacson disliked about his franchisor was that it required the franchisee to buy separate franchises to do different types of cleaning, such as residential carpet cleaning, fire restoration for insurance companies, and commercial cleaning. Isaacson felt it was key to the profitability of a franchisee that he or she be allowed to do a variety of types of cleaning under one franchise.

So Servpro was born!

Another feature he disliked was that his franchisor had a local support staff too few in number and too distant to give each franchisee needed one-on-one assistance. To solve that problem, Servpro developed franchisees who provided franchisee support to other franchisees both on the local and the state levels. These franchisees are paid for their functioning as support staff because they, in turn, receive 60 percent of the royalties from each franchise they service.

"The better the trainers train the franchisees, the more successful the franchisees are and the more money the trainers get," explains Rick Isaacson, Servpro vice-president of marketing and sales.

Servpro's main line of work, constituting 50 percent of its business, is fire and other heavy-duty restoration. This includes damage from floods and other special instances such as when a furnace backs up and spews soot over household contents. This comprehensive service includes water removal, wall cleaning, and floor cleaning, as well as upholstery and drapery cleaning and deodorizing.

Rick Isaacson explains, "Fire restoration can save an insurance company a bundle of money because they no longer have to pay for new furnishings." He notes that Servpro charges only 20 cents a square foot to clean a rug, whereas new carpeting can easily go for $2 a square foot. Likewise, it costs 8 to 12 cents a square foot to clean walls while a professional painter would charge 25 to 35 cents a square foot to repaint. So Servpro saves money in a big way.

But there is more to Servpro.

In 1967, the company began doing residential carpet, upholstery, and drapery cleaning. In 1969, the company started performing that type of cleaning under the Sears name and also had Ethan Allen and Breuner's furniture stores refer customers in recognition of the excellent quality of its service.

During the early 1980s, Servpro expanded its services to commercial cleaning and housecleaning.

In 1986, the company launched a new franchise called Building Service Maintenance, which does just janitorial work. Rick Isaacson states that the separate franchise was set up because janitorial labor requires a different type of worker than does Servpro. More than 60 franchisees have signed up for Building Service Maintenance, half of them existing Servpro franchisees.

Servpro began to offer its highly successful spray-on fire protectant service Inspectashield in 1988. Inspectashield works wonders on any porous surface. In the brief time the service has been on the market, about 75 percent of its customers have been commercial.

Servpro has about 700 franchises in 47 states. The company is now looking to expand into Great Britain and Australia.

Systemwide sales jumped to $65 million for 1988, up 17 percent from a year earlier. Projecting that it will exceed $100 million in annual sales by 1991, Servpro is clearly on the fast track.

The franchise fee is only $32,500, with other start-up costs about $40,000. The royalty is 10 percent for the smallest-volume outlets down to 3 percent for the largest.

Servpro can be a good spare-time venture for entrepreneurs in search of a more substantial business opportunity with a corresponding investment. We found it ideal for people who may be giving up hectic full-time careers but still want a no-nonsense business that can generate a good income with fewer hours.

For more information, write to

Servpro Industries, Inc.
575 Airport Boulevard
Gallatin, TN   37066
(615) 451-0200

WINDOW BLIND CLEANING /
Shine-A-Blind America

There are more than 100 million dirty window blinds in America collecting more dust right this minute. Almost every apartment, home, office, school, factory, or hospital has window blinds, and nobody around to truly clean them professionally.

This is why we think Shine-A-Blind America is one of the hottest business concepts for sideline entrepreneurs today. Not only did Shine-A-Blind find a wide-open market, but it also has put together a terrific concept for reaching and selling its services to this new found market.

Shine-A-Blind starts your success rolling by applying the new technology of ultrasonics to the ordinary chore of removing dirt from window blinds. Using this technique, you can clean blinds using sound waves in approximately 30 seconds. Simple arithmetic will tell you that if you clean 60 blinds at $12 each, you can earn $720. And you can accomplish this in only a few hours!

A winning feature of Shine-A-Blind is that it's a completely portable cleaning system. Drive your truck to your customers, and you won't have to worry about your customers finding you.

The Shine-A-Blind system is easy to learn and operate. It's an ideal opportunity for either men or women, and one that can be operated either part-time or full-time.

Only $13,900 puts you into this lucrative business. For this small investment, you receive state-of-the-art equipment, advertising assistance, and a complete marketing guide. Financing is available, so you can get into this rewarding business with very little money down.

If ever there was a needed service not being performed at this time, blind cleaning is it. Many Shine-A-Blind dealers work only

10–20 hours a week and earn from $600 to $1,000. You can earn substantially more full-time. This is a recession-proof industry, and the demand for this service is constant. Your ability to go directly to your customers is a big advantage over the industry's few competitors who are shackled to a permanent location where customers must find them.

If you talk to Shine-A-Blind dealers as we have, you'll discover for yourself the many reasons window blind cleaning is an excellent business, and why Shine-A-Blind is an excellent company to join forces with.

For more information, write to

Shine-A-Blind America
23310 Van Dyke
Warren, MI   48089
(800) 446-0411

IMPRINTED PRODUCTS /
Signet Systems, Inc.

Imprinted products have become big business. Individuals want personalized products. Imprinted promotional premiums are also a favorite way for companies to keep their name before customers.

Just about anything can be imprinted. Business cards, wedding supplies, matchbooks, diaries, awards, playing cards, key tags—you name it. It doesn't matter whether it's made of glass, wood, metal, plastic, leather, or vinyl. A name, personalized message, or business ad can be imprinted on it with Signet Systems' easy-to-use professional imprinting equipment.

This is a great market because imprinted products are quickly consumed and are constantly being replaced. Once you have a customer you are assured of a steady stream of repeat business. Signet dealers report that as much as 70 percent of their business comes from repeat orders, so once you have a customer you can look forward to a steady stream of dollars.

Because the work is labor-intensive, imprinting is a service of little interest to large commercial competitors. This also means the field is without severe price cutting, thus protecting your profits.

Absolutely no skill or expertise is required to succeed in this business. Company training, including imprinting and marketing techniques, is provided at your own premises. Signet also provides its dealers with an ongoing support program, allowing dealers to benefit from the many new promotional techniques constantly being tested by Signet.

You can earn $35–$65 per hour with your own imprinting service. For example, the profit on one order for 500 business cards can be as high as $45, and the job would take less than one hour to complete. Average profits per order in this business are approximately $30. With only ten orders a week, you can make about $300.

This is one business you can easily operate from your home. But it can also be operated as part of another business, or you can even set up a spare-time imprinting kiosk in shopping malls or other high-traffic locations. The Signet System is an absolute must for any business selling giftware or accessories. Giftware dealers happily admit they can double (even triple) their sales of certain giftware and accessories lines once they offer the imprinting option. Best of all, they can command far higher prices for an imprinted product.

Signet provides the very best imprinting equipment on the market today. You can be in business—complete with training and supplies—for between $5,000 and $10,000.

There are more than 1,200 Signet representatives, so the system has a proven and exciting track record. Signet support is always available and is backed up by more than 12 years' experience, which makes it a leader in this rapidly expanding industry.

For more information, write to

Signet Systems, Inc
50 High Street, Suite LL7
Buffalo, NY   14203
(416) 528-8977
Contact: Ross Connell

NO-SLIP SURFACES / Slipproof Services, Inc.

Here's an astonishing fact: Approximately 1.6 million individuals are disabled by slip or fall accidents each year, and such accidents kill close to 15,000 people in the United States alone.

Steve Sharpe discovered these alarming statistics while attending restaurant and hotel management school, and he decided to do something about it.

"I started with the rough process and materials used by a few pioneers and through the years I've refined the technique into a step-by-step service that can be taught to almost anyone. More importantly, I've packaged the entire business so that distributors can sell the service right in their own communities," says Sharpe.

Sharpe's company is Slipproof Services, Inc., a new distributorship company that evolved from Sharpe Systems, his own service company which since 1983 has solved slipping and falling problems and has satisfied customers ranging from hospitals and jails to national restaurant chains.

The Slipproof process is becoming popular around pools, in kitchens and baths, and on tile and marble floors in residential and commercial settings. Skyrocketing insurance premiums contribute to the boom for Slipproof.

"With my treatment process, slip/fall accidents are a thing of the past. I always tell my customers, 'the wetter, the better it is,'" Sharpe proclaims.

If you are in the sunbelt, you'll have plenty of backyard pools to keep you busy; but we see an equally big Slipproof market among restaurants, whose kitchen employees report wet floors a number one occupational hazard.

The price for an average U.S. market Slipproof distributorship is $12,500, which includes equipment, sales and marketing kits, product supplies, and complete training. In addition,

Sharpe is constantly updating the product line to complement the Slipproof safety system. The latest development is a bathtub coating for homeowners. "We know that 186,000 accidents are bathtub related, and those are only the ones reported, so there is a real need for our product. If we can minimize slip/fall accidents in the homes, then we are succeeding," says Sharpe.

Because Slipproof is such a valuable service, it is in big demand. This means high sales and profits for Slipproof dealers. As a Slipproof dealer you can easily earn $50,000 or more a year—working only two or three days a week. But earnings can really skyrocket once Slipproof catches on. Dealers report, for example, that once Slipproof is installed around a swimming pool, it's only a matter of time before orders begin to come in from friends who, impressed by Slipproof's remarkable antislip properties, want Slipproof for their own pools. The same is true in the restaurant trade, where associations and insurance companies are beginning to recommend Slipproof as a cost-effective way to avoid employee injuries from wet-floor slips.

Competition in this business barely exists, and because the market is so huge, Slipproof can put your future income on a very firm footing.

For more information, write to

Slipproof Services, Inc.
510 Castillo Street
Santa Barbara, CA   93101
(805) 965-5501
(800) 444-0792

PORCELAIN REPAIR AND REFINISHING / Specialty Coatings & Chemicals

Every home, every apartment—virtually every business and institution—has kitchen or bathroom accessories that have become chipped, cracked, stained, or discolored with age. Sometimes they just need a "new look." Until quite recently, anyone with these problems was faced with three alternatives: (1) Replace the entire unit—very often costing two to three times as much to replace as when originally installed (a stiff price to pay for a cracked, chipped, or stained area). (2) Try any of the inadequate "do-it-yourself" concoctions, and possibly end up with rough, unsightly patches of mismatched color—patches that usually crack and discolor even more. (3) Do nothing and let the unsightly problem become progressively worse until you are literally "shamed" into replacing it regardless of cost!

Now there's a new alternative: Special-T Porclynite, a porcelain, tile, ceramic, formica, fiberglass, and marble repair, recoloring, refinishing process with results so perfect the repairs are undetectable!

Special-T Porclynite is not the common everyday two-component epoxy that is difficult to apply with uncontrollable results. Porclynite is, instead, a specially developed polyurethane formulation that virtually becomes "part of" the surface it's applied to, whether it's porcelain, ceramic, or tile. Conceived, developed, tested, manufactured, and proven in Special-T's own laboratories and factory, the Porclynite repair dries quickly and is ready to use. Porclynite has a good wear factor and good resiliency as well as high resistance to fungus, mildew, and the "acids" bathrooms and kitchens are normally subject to.

Now you can make top income (spare-time or full-time) in your very own Porclynite repair/refinishing business.

The giant market includes homes, apartment complexes, motels, hotels, schools, and hospitals. You can assure yourself of a steady income by making contact with large locations on a contract or retainer basis or develop a partnership with builders and plumbing contractors. People want to have their kitchen or bathroom fixtures look like new, avoiding costly repairs and replacement, so you are offering a service with virtually no sales resistance and immediate acceptance.

Porclynite offers significant savings to the customer. For example, a person would have to spend about $1,200 to replace a bathtub. As a Porclynite repair professional, you would charge only $300 to refinish the same bathtub. Thus you offer a customer savings of $900, or 75 percent. But on this same job you could earn $250 to $275 (Porclynite is inexpensive for you to buy), which is a healthy profit for two or three hours' work.

No special skills are needed to profit in your own Porclynite repair/refinishing business. The company provides complete hands-on training and a video training tape to teach you everything you need to know about this easy-to-learn business.

Your earnings potential can range from $25 to $60 an hour. Porclynite dealers report incomes from $20,000 up to $120,000 a year depending on whether they work full- or part-time and how aggressively they market their services.

Your total investment is only $2,300. (An initial payment of only $250 is needed!) Test the great demand for this product on your own. You can start doing repairs on the weekends and keep your existing job, gradually building your successful installation service.

As a Porclynite dealer, you pay no franchise fees or royalties. You pay only for the equipment, training, and supplies. But this doesn't mean you don't have the company's full support. Specialty Coatings excels in dealer support, which is why it is one of the largest and most successful companies in the business.

For more information, write to

Specialty Coatings & Chemicals, Inc.
Dept. BK
7360 Varna Avenue
No. Hollywood, CA   91605
(213) 875-0233
Contact: W. Daniel Ernt

WINDOW TINTING / Specialty Coatings & Chemicals

People everywhere suddenly want their windows tinted to reduce harmful ultraviolet light, reduce glare, and reduce costly heat buildup. This is especially true in the sunbelt, which is the fastest-growing area of the country. The market for window tinting includes cars, trucks, homes, and commercial buildings, so there are an unlimited number of prospective customers for a window-tinting service. As people become even more conscious of the many benefits of window tinting, demand for this service will become enormous.

There are several glass coating products on the market, so why did we choose Special-T's glass coating as the *one* company to join in this fast-growth business? The answer is that Special-T's glass coating tints better than the others.

Special-T's glass coating is like putting giant sunglasses on windows. Special-T's revolutionary coating reduces heat, glare, and fading, and you can actually feel the difference. The exclusive Ultra Violet Absorbing Agent, 2.2, Di-H-4M, creates a filtering action that reduces the UV light up to 98 percent. The UV light is a contributor to fabric fading. It protects displays in store windows, furniture and fabrics in homes, and contents of commercial buildings. And there are no more ugly shades, covers, or awnings to contend with when you install Special-T.

Seven key advantages of Special-T's flow-on glass coatings include

- Flow-on can provide a beautiful seamless tint over the largest windows.

- Flow-on can be applied without any seams on curved windows that curve in two directions.
- Flow-on does not get the bubbles or peeling that is associated with film.
- Properly installed and cared for, flow-on lasts significantly longer than film, without fading. Installations have lasted in excess of 20 years—and still appear like new.
- Window film tears very easily compared to Special-T's liquid glass coating.
- Flow-on raw materials cost less than half that for film, and the inventory is a fraction of that investment. Application cost is approximately 12 cents per square foot—one of the lowest in the industry.
- Flow-on coating "know-how" requires only one or two days' training, and can easily be learned by anyone with basic manual skills.

No special skills are required. The company offers hands-on training plus a video training tape, so you have both initial and continuing support.

Glass tinting offers exceptional earnings potential. (Some operators make $300 an hour in their own glass-tinting business.) Work from 20 to 40 hours a week and watch your income double—even triple!

Special-T welcomes spare-timers because the firm is confident you will quickly become a full-time dealer once you realize how much money you can earn with Special-T's window-tinting service. You can provide the service directly to consumers and work through contractors and builders.

Window tinting is no longer a product exclusively used in warmer climates. The hot rays of the sun can be a big problem in any part of the country, and tinting is now a boom industry in northern states as homes and buildings are converted from plain glass to tinted glass.

Energy conservationists are actively stressing the need for tinting, and doctors warn of the dangers from sun exposure. So people are beginning to understand why they need window tinting, and the demand for this service remains well ahead of the number of qualified installers. This guarantees you a profitable future in your window-tinting business.

For more information, write to

Specialty Coatings & Chemicals, Inc.
Dept. BK
7360 Varna Avenue
No. Hollywood, CA   91605
(213) 875-0233
Contact: W. Daniel Ernt

MERCHANDISE DISTRIBUTORS / Specialty Merchandise Corporation

Specialty Merchandise Corporation (SMC) are importers and big-volume distributors now in search of associates to join the firm in its fast-growth business. SMC deals directly with manufacturers all over the world, buying huge quantities of giftware, jewelry, toys, tools, home and office decor items, novelties, and more. Because SMC buys in such large quantities, it buys at very low prices. Consequently, merchandise is resold to you at fabulous prices that enable you to resell it—even to other wholesalers—and still enjoy a very good profit! Most of SMC's merchandise has a "markup" (the difference between your cost and the retail cost) that ranges from 300 to 1,000 percent. With this huge markup, you're guaranteed a profit no matter how you market the merchandise.

SMC's huge, automated warehouse is now filled with this fast-selling merchandise—more than 3,000 different items at last count, and more great items being added every day! Best of all, working with SMC, you have no customhouse hangups, hard-to-handle paperwork, involved financial arrangements, or unexpected tariff duties to cope with. What's more, you buy only what you need when you need it without costly inventory buildups. Since SMC has no "minimum" orders, you can buy one item, or a thousand, and get the same low, below-wholesale prices!

But SMC does far more than just "sell" you merchandise at very low prices. It literally "puts you in your own profitable business" by supplying easy-to-follow, step-by-step business plans, plus all the "backup" material you need to make the program work for you—including full-color product catalogs, complete with suggested selling prices.

Of course, if everybody liked to do business the same way, SMC could offer just one "catch-all" selling plan. But fortunately, everybody isn't the same. Different people have different personalities. Some like nothing better than to get out and sell personally. Others shrink from direct sales.

SMC's solution to this problem is to offer you a wide variety of business plans. As soon as you enroll, SMC sends you a business kit, complete with plans for each of the 21 different ways you can distribute merchandise profitably. These plans range all the way from mail order (where you hardly ever see your customers) to party plans and flea markets (where you meet and sell to your customers eyeball to eyeball).

Don't worry about making a "choice," however. They send you all the complete programs. They are yours to keep—every one of them! Study each of them, and pick the one you think is best suited for you. Or even pick two or three or more—as many as you want. You're not "locked in" to any one program. You can change programs back and forth or try new programs as often as you wish. SMC's business and advisory staff is always available to help you with your marketing questions or problems. There is no charge for this service.

SMC membership is not a franchise. You operate under your own firm name. You are not assessed for advertising costs or expected to pay a percentage of profits. All the money you make is your own.

SMC prices are sometimes one-half (or less) of those charged by other distributors and importers. Your profits reach to five times your cost or more! Only SMC members can buy from SMC at SMC's lowest below-wholesale jobber prices. Only SMC members can avail themselves of the benefits, sales programs, instruction, and other aids that assure success if the SMC program is followed with dedication.

Any SMC plan can be started in your spare time. If you wish, you may continue it as a full-time business as soon as the profits equal your present salary.

For more than 40 years, SMC has helped over 40,000 others realize their dreams of independence —and they can do the same for you.

For more information, write to

Specialty Merchandise Corporation
Dept. 477-07
9401 DeSoto Avenue
Chatsworth, CA   91311-4991
(818) 998-3300

INSTANT SIGN SERVICE / Spectrum Signs Corporation

In years past, signs were a dirty, messy proposition, painted by hand by artisans in dingy, back-of-the-warehouse locations. And ordinary signs sold at exorbitant prices.

Now, through creative attention to modern marketing techniques coupled with state-of-the-art computer graphics and photographic technology, Spectrum Signs Corporation has created America's first total Instant Sign service and has revolutionized the sign industry. This turnkey business is a neat, clean, Main Street business, completely automated, offering next-day service on a wide variety of commercial signs and banners that businesses use on a repetitive basis.

The instant-sign industry is four years old and just beginning. Destined to be the instant-print industry equivalent of the 1990s, this can be your opportunity to get in on the ground floor. If you are a person with vision and are willing to work hard for success, or if you have ever wished you had foreseen opportunity and had joined a proven industry on the ground floor but missed out, don't miss out this time!

Spectrum Signs Corporation offers a comprehensive, professional business in which each product line feeds the others and where the entire system is driven by aggressive, modern marketing. Spectrum is a complete business package that includes marketing, technical training, and all the necessary ongoing support that has, until now, only been available through very expensive franchises.

Operating your own Spectrum Signs service (either full- or part-time), you can offer outdoor signs and banners, in-store signage, paper-laminated banners, interior building signs, magnetic vehicle signs, vinyl lettering—just about any size or type of sign you can possibly think of.

And because you have available the widest variety, fastest service, and highest quality, you can understand why Spectrum is revolutionizing the entire sign business and why Spectrum Signs store owners are so successful.

As a Spectrum Instant Signs store owner, you receive complete initial training. (Anyone can make beautiful signs with Spectrum's easy method.) You also receive a network newsletter, yellow pages ad slicks, a toll-free 800 support line, direct mail pieces, target telemarketing, store layout design, network meetings, network discounts on supplies, public relations guidelines, and the experience of the industry leaders.

Why not consider your own automated instant sign store (or even mini-chain) to provide businesses in your community with quality signs in only 24 hours? Absentee ownership is very possible.

No painting or other skills are necessary to produce beautiful signs with the Spectrum system. The easy-to-operate equipment automatically creates professional signs with a push of a few buttons.

Spectrum Signs Corporation sends a real message to you if you want your own permanent business with profit power!

For more information, write to

Spectrum Signs Corporation
424 NW Third Street
P.O. Box 731
Brainerd, MN   56401
(800) 328-3453

SPORTING GOODS AND APPAREL /
Sport It, Inc.

America is shaping up! And in the process Americans are spending more money than ever before to purchase athletic and fitness products to become healthier and happier and to gain a competitive spirit. The sporting goods and apparel business has become a $20 billion industry almost overnight!

Growth means opportunity—opportunity that could help you become part of this exciting athletic and fitness industry. And Sport It may just be the kind of opportunity you've been seeking.

Sport It specializes in the planning and development of Sport It authorized dealers who sell athletic and fitness products to a large and ready market.

Here's how it works: On joining their program, you gain access to a nearly unlimited selection of sporting goods and sportswear merchandise that you can sell to virtually any individual or organization interested in sports and fitness activities—at prices that are competitive with retailers in your area. You have immediate access to sporting goods, sportswear, and related services that include the best brand names in the industry.

With Sport It you instantly have the ability to meet the needs and demands of consumers for a wide variety of sports activities, including baseball and softball, basketball, volleyball, football, golf, cheerleading, jogging, soccer, and tennis, to name just a few.

Sport It authorized dealers have access to virtually every type of lettering and imprinting service, including silk screening, chainstitching, embroidery, and heat transfers.

Quality trophies, plaques, ribbons, and other types of awards are available at the lowest possible prices and with fast delivery service. Customized engraving services with superior craftsmanship are also available, so you can become a full-service representative.

From grade schools to campus bookstores, there's a great need for sports-related items in educational institutions. Warm-ups, shirts, uniforms, athletic equipment, playground equipment, physical education equipment and supplies, trophies, awards, and jackets are all items that are needed in schools.

Rotary, Kiwanis, Lions, Masons, and other organizations commonly purchase apparel as well as plaques and trophies. Such associations may also sponsor athletic teams—another good source of business.

As a Sport It authorized dealer, you can distribute catalogs provided by sporting goods suppliers to a targeted group of customers. Your customers gain the convenience of shopping at home, and you increase your sales with minimal effort.

The home-party concept of sales mixes fun with business, which is the perfect atmosphere for sporting goods. It provides an opportunity to make new business contacts while displaying featured items for special promotions.

As a Sport It authorized dealer, you are your own boss and you make your own business decisions. You set your own hours and work at your own pace. You can even run your business right from your home.

Your potential earnings as a Sport It authorized dealer are tremendous. Your potential market is virtually unlimited. Men and women, young and old, individuals and organizations, friends and relatives, co-workers and acquaintances—all are potential buyers of sporting goods.

No specific skills or training is needed. However, individuals must have the desire and ability to succeed in their own business.

Sport It offers dealers free training seminars, free consultation, training manuals and audio tapes, monthly newsletters, annual conventions, and numerous support services and programs.

There are nearly 2,200 Sport It dealers happily making money, but there's plenty of room for more. This high-profit opportunity can be yours for the low start-up cost of only $1,500.

For more information, write to

Sport It, Inc.
8960 Springbrook Dr. NW, Suite 150
Minneapolis, MN   55433
(612) 784-0490
(800) 328-3820
Contact: Rick Hartman

"TALKING" BALLOON SALES / Talking Balloons, Inc.

Here's a crazy, crazy new product to sell, and one that can bring out the sun on even a cloudy day! This blockbuster is the one and only Talking Balloon.

That's right, these balloons really *do* talk! You can actually hear them talking, and so can the people around you! People laugh when you show them a Talking Balloon that says "Hello Sweetheart," "I love you," or "Kiss me, you fool"! Or for someone's birthday it could say, "Happy Birthday" and then laugh "Ha! Ha! Ha!" There are more than 75 different things Talking Balloons can say, including a few that can make a marine blush!

How do "Talking" Balloons talk?

Imagine a red two-foot-long string (or ribbon) that is specially made like a record. The ribbon is prerecorded with little grooves much like a record has. When you attach it to anything that is thin or hollow, like a balloon or box, you can make it talk and say things like "Happy Birthday!" or "Thanks for your business!" This is an excellent way to get a message across for personal or business needs, wouldn't you agree?

Talking Balloons sell themselves at football games, concerts, shopping malls, flea markets, or wherever there are people to be fascinated. Deliver Talking Balloon Bouquets for Valentine's Day and Mother's Day and watch the smiles. Earn thousands more just by selling Talking Balloons to virtually every type of retailer, including convenience stores, department stores, florists, balloon shops, car dealerships, novelty shops, and even the ad specialty markets. Start from home and expand as you grow! The possibilities with Talking Balloons are unlimited.

Because Talking Balloons can be prerecorded with so many varied messages, schools successfully use them as fund raisers (say, "Go Team Go!"). Businesses increasingly use Talking Balloons as an advertising tool, so you can easily target different markets.

Use them for political slogans, fund raising, and trade show exhibitors. Instead of a Talking Balloon, how about putting the talking ribbon on a box and sell Talking Pizza Boxes to a pizza company? See what we mean when we say unlimited possibilities!

Talking Balloons is a fun and profitable business. The opportunity is being offered to you, right now, for the first time! All markets are wide open and practically untouched. Start by purchasing a $348 starter package with enough Talking Balloons to gross you $1,415. That's nearly a 400 percent profit.

Or start by purchasing a sample demo package of only two complete Talking Balloons. You'll love the demos. Each one has eight different sayings to titillate you.

Talking Balloons shows you how to set up in shopping malls, whom to talk to, and how to sell at sporting events, fund raisers, corporate accounts, and more! This is a ground-floor opportunity! Don't wait until Talking Balloons are all over your town. Be the one to put them there!

Talking Balloons is a fun-packed business. It's almost like being in the entertainment business.

If you've been looking for a business that has tremendous upside potential, with very little risk, you've found it with Talking Balloons.

For more information, write to

Talking Balloons, Inc.
6735 Peachtree Industrial Boulevard
Suite 105, Dept. 1
Atlanta, GA   30360
(404) 449-7898
(800) 328-2551
Contact: Chris Parker

HOME-BASED GIFT BASKETS / Tara Perkins
Baskets

Christmas. Birthdays. Anniversaries. The calendar year is full of special occasions when people search for that "perfect gift." That's where gift baskets come in—baskets filled with special goodies, each with a special theme to delight the recipient and fatten the wallets of those with the creativity for this new and exciting business.

This cottage industry has captured the attention of entrepreneurs all over America, and if you have a flair for creativity and marketing techniques, you too can turn ordinary wicker baskets into beautiful and useful gifts—and be well rewarded for your efforts.

The gift basket business has a practically unlimited market, because a gift basket can adopt a theme for just about any occasion. One example is a "new baby" basket loaded with baby-care items and toys to delight the newborn. Another is a "tea time" basket appropriate for any occasion or simply to let the recipient know you are thinking of him or her. Of course, fruit and candy baskets remain perennial favorites, but some operators have become imaginative enough to put together graduation baskets filled with items relating to the graduate's new career or future plans.

These small baskets do produce big, big profits. A typical gift basket may cost as little as $5 but may retail for $45 or even more. And because demand is both constant and growing, even a spare-time gift basket service can gross $120,000 annually with very little overhead. This is one business you can easily operate from your kitchen table. Just think about it—selling an average of only 10 baskets per day at an average price of $35 to $50 can mean substantial profits of nearly $100,000 a year.

To succeed in this business, you must first know the tricks to properly start and promote your business so you can tap it for its greatest potential. That's where Tara Perkins Baskets comes in. Tara Perkins publishes a practical and comprehensive manual that has become the bible for building a basket business. With this manual at your fingertips, you will find a wealth of information—on everything you need to know to start and succeed in your own "gift basket service," including

- Where to find the inventory you need, at the lowest possible price
- How to design and assemble irresistible baskets to keep you far ahead of the competition
- How to sell baskets both at retail and through a delivery service
- How to capture those ultraprofitable corporate accounts
- How to price your baskets for top profit
- How to promote your business at small cost
- And much, much more.

This is truly a business opportunity within a book—and it can be your full-time armchair adviser for only $18.95.

Join in the happiness of creating fast-selling gift baskets. You can easily begin for several hours a week and gradually build it to as large a business as you choose.

It costs very little to start your own spare-time gift basket business. Many successful operators began with less than a $2,000 investment. And it's a repeat business. Customers will come back to you time and time again for that perfect gift.

For more information, write to

Tara Perkins Baskets
2796 Harbor Boulevard, #107
Costa Mesa, CA   92626
(714) 645-5696

TUTORING SERVICE / Top Marks Learning Network

Tutoring is a service business with an uncommonly high profit structure in a fabulous growth market. More than that, your facility requirements and equipment needs are so tiny in comparison to many other service businesses that they're almost negligible. That adds up to good news for a tutoring operation with something to teach the market.

Top Marks can put you into the tutoring business with its new and exceptionally profitable tutoring concept. As a tutoring counselor, you match students who need tutoring with teachers and other qualified tutors willing to provide tutoring services during their own spare-time hours.

There are thousands of students in every area. Top Marks covers all subjects from elementary grades through graduate school. Tutoring is even provided for languages, music, computers, and SAT and other preparatory tests. Teachers are also easy to find because so many teachers are looking to earn additional income.

What can you earn with your own Top Marks agency? Earnings of $500–$600 a week placing an average of 50 students is realistic. Overseeing that activity shouldn't take more than six to eight hours a week. And you can earn considerably more if you provide tutoring services yourself.

Anyone can easily learn and operate this business. (It's ideal for teachers.) Top Marks gives you a complete instruction manual, ongoing consultation, a proven marketing program, and all the forms and operational material you'll need.

Tutoring is big business, but only Top Marks offers a proven way for nonteachers to cash in on this tremendous market. You are provided with all the marketing material needed to attract both students and tutors, which is especially easy to do since there is an abundance of both students in need of tutors and tutors anxious to add to their income by tutoring. (Their mutual problem before Top Marks was formed was that they had no organized way to find each other.) With the Top Marks system you assign the students to the tutor, bill the student for each lesson, collect the tuition, and remit to the tutor *after* you have been paid. So you stay in control of the funds every step of the way. Your share is one-third of the tuition charge (or about $5 per one-hour lesson, although rates vary depending on market and subject).

Top Marks is a complete system. You receive all the agreements, student record forms, sample correspondence, and an information-packed manual on how to successfully operate every phase of the business.

You can offer a Top Marks service in just about any locality. Even small towns with populations of less than 20,000 can comfortably support a Top Marks because it offers tutoring over such a wide range of subjects.

To join the Top Marks team, you need only good organizational skills and a one-time start-up fee of $495 to cover training and all materials. There are no franchise fees or royalties; you keep all the income as profit.

Although Top Marks is a new company, it promises to be one of the fastest-growth opportunities of the decade because it is a company staffed by professional educators with a proven track record in the tutoring business.

For more information, write to

Top Marks Learning Network
366 SE Fifth Avenue
Delray Beach, FL   33483
(407) 243-3701

DISCOUNT TRAVEL CLUB / Travel Club International

Would you like the opportunity to save travelers up to 60 percent on *all* their travel costs? That's right. Your customers can enjoy blockbuster discounts on all major air carriers, over 1,000 cruises, hotels, car rentals—you name it, even travel insurance! And what if you could earn $109 profit on each $129 membership you sell? Doesn't that sound like a terrific wealth-building deal? Of course. We thought so, too, and that's why we investigated and included Travel Club International as one of the *100 Best*.

But it's all true. All you have to do is sell $129 memberships in Travel Club International (TCI) and you pocket $109 on every sale made. After all, who would pass up the chance to save so much on their travel needs for a paltry $129?

Travel Club International does just about everything once you sell the membership. The firm provides exclusive territories, so you are without competition. Your customers are ticketed through TCI's accredited travel offices. The firm even sponsors a 24-hour hot line, so you have the latest in travel bargains at your fingertips. Travel Club International also provides membership cards, handbooks, a complete training manual, ad slicks, and everything else you need for a first-rate marketing program. There are even color brochures available with your private label for your customers.

Membership in Travel Club International is a fabulous sales premium. For example, you can sell multiple membership packages to car lots, health clubs, time-share resorts, and anyone else who could use a powerful premium of discount travel privileges to sell a product or service.

Consider the earnings potential of this business. If you sell just one membership a day, you can earn $32,700 a year. Five memberships and you gross $327,000.

You can become a TCI representative without any investment on your part. Pick your own hours. Keith and Lee Monen, who founded Travel Club International, have discovered a way to go from poverty to wealth almost overnight with this program. Although we cannot guarantee you'll become wealthy selling TCI memberships, it does look to us like a way to sell an extremely attractive product at a tremendous profit.

If you would like to check out this opportunity in greater detail, why not first become a Travel Club International member yourself? Then you can see how many different ways *you* can save on your next vacation or business trip. Once you discover the fabulous savings, you can sell club memberships with enthusiasm, and this is the key to enrolling the small armies of members that can truly make you rich. A direct membership is only $20—a sum you can recoup perhaps 50 times over on your next vacation trip alone.

Travel Club International can help you say *au revoir* to being broke and *bonjour* to making big money in the travel business.

For more information, write to

Travel Club International
3052 El Cajon Boulevard
San Diego, CA   92104
(619) 273-2202

IMPRINTABLE SPORTSWEAR SHOPS /
T-Shirts Plus

You just knew a T-shirt shop had to be included in the *100 Best* because T-shirts have grown into a steady multi-million dollar business. Just about everyone—from 6 to 60—has one or more T-shirts emblazoned with some perky or naughty message. The market is expected to grow rapidly as T-shirts become accepted attire at all but the fanciest places. And what can be more comfortable—or inexpensive—than a wardrobe of T-shirts for every occasion?

If you can see your future in T-shirts, why not consider joining forces with T-Shirts Plus—the clear winner among scores of T-shirt retailing franchises now cashing in on this booming market.

T-Shirts Plus knows about teamwork; there are now about 200 happy franchisees nationwide. And they have the snappiest line of T-shirts and sportswear we have come across—T-shirts that will move out of your store in droves.

There are plenty of real pluses with T-Shirts Plus. The company can help you find and negotiate leases in the best malls. (This is one business that depends on location, location, location.) It also provides complete leasing and construction assistance, and a high-tech, new store design for that super-smart image. Cash requirements are as low as $25,000, and financing assistance is available.

You can achieve financial independence with a T-Shirt Plus shop—and it's a business you can easily oversee in your spare time.

How much you can make depends, of course, on location and your own efforts, but T-Shirts Plus will give you just about everything you can need to double or even triple your current income.

Some T-Shirts Plus operators pull in incomes in excess of $50,000 annually. Even on a part-time (or absentee) basis, you can take home sizable profits because overhead is low, low, low in this business. Mark-ups are high; you can buy on the best terms and prices when you are part of the T-Shirts Plus family.

You can sell T-shirts anywhere, in any market. Demand is consistently strong, and T-shirts are a terrific impulse item (particularly in resort or beach areas). T-shirts can even be marketed by mail or by catalog (particularly with the colorful T-Shirt Plus line). *Income Opportunities* (October, 1988) predicts T-shirt sales will *double* in the next five years. This means significant profits for entrepreneurs already established in the best locations.

It's hard to beat T-Shirts Plus' combination of great-looking shirts, sharp retail decor, and set-up and marketing support. But why try?

For more information, write to

T-Shirts Plus
3630 1H-35 South
Waco, TX   76706
(800) 634-9607

SNACK FOOD SERVICE / United Snack Group, Inc.

Have you ever noticed "on-your-honor" snack displays at local places of business? Perhaps there are snack racks loaded with sandwiches, candy, cookies, soft drinks, and assorted other goodies available where you work. You may never have thought about it, but there are enormous profits to be made from all those nickels, dimes, and quarters tossed into the cup by hungry employees and customers.

United Snack Group, Inc., a leader in the snack food field, knows how popular these snack racks can be. United Snack's problem is that there are too many prospective accounts but too few people to handle the business. Rather than turn away customers, United Snack wisely turned to franchising as a way to serve this enormous market.

As a snack food franchisee, you will enjoy a protected territory of no fewer than 1,500 accounts. To start you off right, United Snack guarantees placement of the first 550 displays and handles all sales to fully develop your territory until it reaches its 1,500-account potential.

Your job is to service your territory, which means delivery to your accounts from a small, local warehouse. Two employees are needed for each 500 customers serviced, so it's a relatively easy business to oversee even when fully developed.

The snack food market is virtually untapped. Ninety-five percent of all U.S. businesses cannot support an on-premises commissary and depend on self-serve snack systems (such as those offered by United Snacks) as the most practical way to provide packaged foods to employees.

This is one business you can easily operate in fewer than 40 hours a week, although fully developed territories may demand full-time attention. You can make between $30,000 and $150,000 a year, again depending on the number and volume of your accounts and the number of hours you elect to work each week.

Snack foods are an all-cash business, so you have no receivables to contend with. Inventory is limited and mark-ups are huge, giving you an excellent cash flow. Because this is so easy a business to operate, it has good absentee potential. Your investment in United Snacks is $65,000, which includes all inventory, supplies, start-up costs, and a $20,000 franchise fee.

Full training is provided by United Snack; however, there is very little for you to learn because United Snack handles most of the work. This business is suitable for men or women of any age and background. The franchise cost may seem a little steep, but it's really quite reasonable when you realize most of the cost is backed by inventory and that potential earnings are so high. Earnings are also quite stable, because all sales are repeat sales to existing accounts. The beauty of this business is its simplicity. It's simple to get into, simple to operate, and simple to make money with. Our reasons for selecting United Snack is as simple as that.

For more information, write to

United Snack Group, Inc.
1821 University Avenue, N350
St. Paul, MN   55104
(800) 535-9977
Contact: Ed Klein

SELF-HELP VIDEOTAPES / Universal Marketing Company

Several thousand video programs characterize what the video industry refers to as the "Special Interest" category. With these self-help tapes you can learn everything from shooting a hole-in-one to losing weight, playing piano to building a birdhouse. In many respects these video programs represent American television at its very best. Yet, until now, there has been no single source where the viewing public could find out what tapes were available, much less actually purchase special-interest tapes for themselves or their families.

The potential market for self-help tapes is unlimited: More than 60 percent of American households now own VCRs. So prolific is this $3.3 billion video industry, businesses that sell and rent videos are expected to thrive for generations to come.

Video Magalog and the World of Winners are the first to bring together the best "self-help" producers in the video industry and to sell these tapes to the mass market through multi-level marketing (MLM).

Their company, Universal Marketing, is actively looking for independent distributors in different areas to contact video stores, book stores, TV–VCR stores, supermarkets, drug stores, churches, schools, libraries, and fund raisers that, in turn, could effectively market their catalogs. Self-help video catalogs sell for $2.95, and each catalog comes with a discount certificate for $2.95 to cover a first purchase, so the catalog is free to the customer as soon as he or she orders!

As a distributor, you would also sponsor stores as dealers. This is a *dual income opportunity* for the stores and organiza-

215

tions. Not only do the stores earn from Magalog sales, but they also earn an added bonus of a 15 percent commission on *any* videos ordered from the catalog in their store.

Look how you can pyramid your income. As a distributor you would receive a 5 percent commission on *any* videos purchased from *any* catalog from *any* stores you sponsor—*forever*! The opportunity is incredible; the potential is unlimited!

You can also sponsor other distributors and receive a 2 percent override on *any* volume they create, four levels down!

The MLM program works like this: Let's say, for example, you sponsor a videotape rental store near your home. The owner signs a dealer application and pays $25 for a dealer's kit which includes a countertop display rack and 12 Video Magalog catalogs. The dealer sells the catalogs for a profit and is paid a commission of 15 percent on any tapes ordered by his or her customers. Commissions are paid monthly, and catalogs are revised and updated every three months. Each catalog retails for $2.95 and, as already noted, includes a $2.95 discount coupon and a Magalog subscription envelope. Each catalog is personalized with the dealer's name and MLM distributor's ID number for proper commission accounting. You, as the dealer's sponsor, would receive a 5 percent commission on anything purchased from the same catalog. You can also sell or give away the catalogs and receive the dealer's 15 percent commission. You also receive a 2 percent commission on all volume from other distributors in your downline.

Remember, you will be marketing a product in very high demand. No inventory is required and accounts are established for life. You receive overrides on your distributors, so income is virtually unlimited!

With Universal you don't waste time constantly searching for new accounts to make a sale. Once you have a good sales base, you receive a generous income ($500 to $800 a week spare-time doesn't raise eyebrows in this business), much as you would from an annuity.

Write today to Universal for a copy of the catalog. You'll see how Universal's tapes have something for just about everybody, including some cash-raising possibilities for you.

For more information, write to

Universal Marketing Company
7631 N. Massingale Place
Tucson, AZ   85741
(602) 744-9313
Contact: Richard Hestad

DESIGN WALLPRINTING / The Unwallpaper Co.

You are about to discover a revolution in wall painting and decorating. Design painting is going to change the way people think about their walls. The profit potential is exciting, and you can be among the first in the business.

Rarely does a new business opportunity come along with such a vast untouched market. Every home, office, hotel or motel, apartment and office building, school, hospital, nursing home, factory, and store—in fact, *every wall in America*—is the market for design wallprinting!

In the home and office, design wallprinting offers the beauty of wallpaper for less than the price of an ordinary paint job. This is because wallprinting hides dirt, marks, and spots that would easily show up on a plain painted wall, so the wall does not require frequent repainting and results in a net savings in the long run. Wallprinting will easily last two or three times longer than an ordinary paint job.

Besides being less expensive than plain paint, design painting is actually better than wallpaper because there are no seams to peel apart, it cannot tear, and it never needs to be steamed off. To redecorate you just repaint. Since design painting uses ordinary paint, it cannot harm the wall; it is ideal in apartments where the leases often do not permit wallpaper. It's a great way to decorate because every design can be applied in any color to match the customer's taste or color scheme.

Design wallprinting works in places where wallpaper cannot be applied at all, such as on textured walls, cinder blocks, or bricks, or in buildings where the fire code requires the use of fire-retardant paints. Your customers will be asking for design wallprinting not only in the traditional wallpaper places such as kitchens and baths, but in every room in the house, because wallprinting creates decorator bedrooms, elegant dining rooms, fabulous living rooms, charming nurseries, and very practical children's playrooms.

Office space and the commercial and industrial sector represent yet another vast market for design painting. Consider the problem faced by hotel and motel owners. They must offer rooms that are attractive, easy to clean, and inexpensive to redecorate. Plain painted walls are not very attractive, and they require frequent repainting. Wallpaper is attractive, but it is also very expensive. The solution is design wallprinting—a coating that is attractive, inexpensive, and easy to maintain.

Design wallprinting can offer something else that wallpaper cannot—a graffiti-proof surface. A design-painted wall can actually be treated with a hard, tile-like coating that meets all government specifications for use in the most demanding areas such as hospitals, nursing homes, and even food processing locations. A number of people are actually beginning to specialize in offering graffiti-proof designed surfaces for high-traffic locations that require attractiveness and cleanliness. They seem to have a corner on this lucrative market. Incidentally, a graffiti-proof coating can be applied to cinder block as well to create the appearance of beautiful decorator tiles! The training manual tells you how it's done.

We cannot predict how successful you might become, but we do get reports that wallprinters are experiencing a great deal of success. Although some are content to operate a part-time wallprinting business, others have given up their jobs to go into wallprinting full-time, and still others have become so successful they now employ several full-time crews.

The arithmetic works something like this. Design painters are getting $100–$150 per room just to put on the design itself. Since such a job should take no more than about two hours (including preparation and clean-up), it works out to a gross profit of $50–$75 per hour. *Entrepreneur* magazine (November, 1988) reported a gross of $72 per hour with a potential high net profit of $60,000 per year before taxes. Not a bad return for a spare-time (or full-time) business you can start for about $1,500.

One of the most remarkable things about wallprinting is that it uses so little paint. An entire 9×12 room can be design painted using only about a half-quart of paint, which should cost no more than $3–$5 per room. With such small overhead expenses, nearly the entire gross profit goes right down to the bottom line!

One of the nicest things about the wallprinting business is how easy it is to get started. You don't have to become a door-to-door salesperson with this service. A small newspaper advertisement with an illustration of a wallprinting machine in operation will bring in more requests for estimates than you can handle. Similarly, a small ad placed in the wallpaper section of the Yellow Pages will bring inquiries from persons who are considering wallpaper, but who would consider this beautiful alternative to wallpaper once they know it is available. There are even ways to generate business without advertising, such as sending out press releases, demonstrating the item at malls and county fairs, and mailing flyers to neighborhoods and businesses.

Learning design wallprinting is not difficult at all. All you need is the right kind of equipment, the right know-how, and a little practice. The firm provides you with the first two items, and you provide the last. The patented equipment comes with its own traction wheels, which ensure jitter-free and slip-proof operation even on slick surfaces such as semi-gloss and high-gloss walls. With the benefit of the extensive training manual as a guide, you can become a qualified wallprinter in your own home in about one week.

For more information, write to

The Unwallpaper Co.
Box 757
Silver Spring, MD   20901
(301) 589-5887

DRIVE-THRU VIDEO RENTALS / Vidtron, Inc.

You wanted to watch *Jaws,* but the video has already been rented. So has *A Fish Called Wanda.* Ditto for *Die Hard.*

Let's face it, by the time you get to the video store, the hot films are gone. You're forced to make a choice between *Red Sonja* and *Transylvania 6-5000.* It's another evening of "ho-hum" movies.

You're not alone.

Two million times a week, movie-hungry Americans walk into video rental stores and discover that the one title they want is long gone from the shelf. *Video Digest* reports that only 12 percent of video customers actually find the specific film they're looking for. Still, Americans rent 120 million tapes a week, and many settle for their second, third, or even fourth choice.

Vidtron founder and co-owner, Michael Grozier, says his own frustration as a video renter led to his brainstorm that spawned his Texas-based business.

"We were renting movies from a local store when I noticed that, regardless of the size business, only a small section of the store was devoted to new releases," Grozier says.

"I also noticed that, no matter how many people were in the store, they all crowded into that one little section featuring hit movies."

Convinced that video rental is far from the "fad" it was once thought to be, Grozier set out to develop a new concept in video outlets that cater exclusively to new releases and proven hits. Convenience, he decided, was the second key component in the design of this radical newcomer to the video scene—called Vidtron.

So, in April 1986, with 97 tapes stocked in an old Fotomat kiosk in Cleburne, Texas, Grozier opened the nation's first of a soon-to-be chain of drive-thru video stores.

Grozier reports the concept was a smash hit from the start. As many as 20 cars line up to rent movies from the store's drive-up window most nights, causing constant traffic jams.

"After just two to three weeks, we increased our inventory to 160 tapes because demand was so terrific," says Grozier. "By the third weekend, we were such a hit, I rented all but six tapes. My shelves were empty but my cash register was full."

The Vidtron kiosk, with its 6' × 8' interior, is designed with double drive-up windows and space to accommodate two workers. It's small but efficient.

Once inventory reached 200 tapes, Grozier realized he had to find a way to unload tapes no longer in demand.

"For us, the tape market is like the stock market," says Grozier. "We keep a tape only as long as it produces for us, then we sell it. With such limited space, we can't afford to keep tapes around that 'might' rent. We look for the sure thing. That's the real key to our success."

Vidtron generally stocks tapes for 45–60 days. When popularity wanes, the movies are resold to a secondary market—generally video wholesalers.

Grozier claims it's the drive-thru aspect of his store that has made it a real hit with customers.

"I hear so many women say they're glad they can rent tapes without leaving their car, dragging the kids into a store behind them," Grozier says. "If you've been out working on the lawn and don't want to change clothes, or if the weather's bad, the Vidtron drive-thru concept is also a blessing."

Grozier says people have been urging him to sell Vidtron franchises almost since the company's inception, but it wasn't until June 1988 that he finalized plans and placed the first ad outlining the Vidtron franchise opportunity.

"We really wanted to make sure we were on firm footing and had all the kinks worked out before we involved other people," Grozier admits.

Vidtron has divided the nation into 50 regions, each with populations of about 2 million people. For $100,000, an individual can buy the rights to a particular region. That person, in turn, can sell franchises within the region and can keep 80 percent of the $12,500 franchise fee from each franchise within his territory.

The Vidtron franchise fee covers a one-week training program, and information on buying tapes, advertising, employment management, bookkeeping, and other operating strategies.

Grozier estimates that franchisees spend another $17,500–$27,500 for their building, inventory, rental, insurance, legal assistance, and first month's payroll.

"Vidtron isn't about to sell franchises and then leave the franchisees out in the cold," says Grozier. "We will always be there, supplying demographic studies, lists of movies to stock, and most importantly, our strength, support and experience as the first . . . and largest in this new niche in the video rental business."

Vidtron can be successfully operated spare-time. Most of the business is done during late afternoons, evenings, and weekends, so you can keep a job provided its hours are relatively short. The work is pleasant and the business is easily operated by men or women of any age.

How much can *you* make from your own Vidtron? That's the $64,000 question. Why not ask the folks at Vidtron? They'll give you some answers that'll make you mighty glad you asked.

For more information, write to

Vidtron, Inc.
105-C West Meadow
Cleburne, TX   76031
(817) 556-3888

CARPET, UPHOLSTERY, AND WALL CLEANING / Von Schrader Co.

It's more fact than cliché to say that Von Schrader Associates are really cleaning up. Von Schrader is the only company with three great business opportunities in one—carpet cleaning, upholstery cleaning, and wall cleaning—so you can now offer your customers a *total* cleaning service that is both remarkably efficient and profitable!

The market for these related services is truly unlimited. Wherever you look, in virtually every commercial or residential building, there is carpet and furniture to be cleaned, and, of course, all have walls and ceilings that get dirty. It's a growing multi-billion dollar business because technology in the manufacture of carpet and fabrics is changing at an increasingly rapid rate, calling for new cleaning materials to be produced and new profit potential for cleaners to be realized.

Von Schrader excels at what it does because its equipment is state-of-the-art. In carpet cleaning, for example, the Dry Foam Extraction System of cleaning leaves carpets deeply cleaned but dry for use in only one to two hours—a highly desirable feature. The system is safe because very little moisture is involved, so water problems frequently associated with other systems can't occur. Equipment is light, portable, and easy to use correctly, and this cleaning method has high customer acceptance. The Dry Foam Upholstery Extractor System is equally safe and thorough for even the more exotic and difficult-to-clean fabrics. This equipment is also portable and involves a special methodology found in no other cleaning system. It's so easy to use that people particularly enjoy working with it.

Each business package is a complete self-contained program. The price includes machines of exclusive, patented design to perform a superior cleaning service, along with sufficient supplies to get the business well off the ground. Supplies furnished include chemicals, advertising materials, a comprehensive business development manual, and complete instructions, enabling you to start earning exceptional income immediately!

You can purchase each program separately if you prefer. The carpet cleaning program is only $2,695; upholstery cleaning is just $2,375; and $1,300 for the wall cleaning system is a bargain. Some financial assistance is available to qualified buyers. There are no other costs other than replacement costs for supplies. There are no royalties, system payments, or fees of any kind, because Von Schrader wants you to keep all the profits. There are no contracts or exclusive territories.

Written instructions supplied with each business are so complete and thorough that no special skills or training is required to professionally operate any of the Von Schrader systems. However, a no-charge 2 1/2-day training school is available on an optional attendance basis for those who prefer hands-on training.

Each service is capable of providing an income of $30–$40 per hour for service work performed at average service prices. However, it is not unusual to gross in excess of $50,000 the first year in business. Working even spare-time (15–25 hours a week) can add more than $700 to your weekly income.

The two main benefits of Von Schrader deserve repeating. First, with Von Schrader you can offer a *complete* cleaning program. Customers no longer have to call in separate services to clean their carpets, ceilings, and walls. Not only do customers find the Von Schrader service a more convenient service, but you have the opportunity to cross-sell your services, effectively tripling your income and productivity.

Second, with Von Schrader you have the very *best* cleaning service on the market. You will find it easier to work with this service, and customers will appreciate the superior results.

For more information, write to

Von Schrader Co.
Dept. BK
1600 Junction Avenue
Racine, WI   53403
(414) 634-1956
Contact: Herb Meyer or Len Gultch

LOAN BROKERAGE / Wes-State Mortgage, Inc.

Wes-State Mortgage, Inc., a leading national loan brokerage firm, is looking for people to join it in this lucrative business as professional loan brokers, associate brokers, or private lenders.

You can earn big money as a loan broker, and the folks at Wes-State prove it each and every day by bringing lenders together with people in search of real estate or business financing.

Fifteen years ago, loan brokers were virtually unknown. Today, almost all borrowers turn to brokers to present their loan proposals. Why? Because borrowers are often turned down by their local banks and lending institutions, and therefore, they turn to brokers when financing becomes more difficult to locate.

Wes-State works closely with lending institutions throughout the nation and can accept any type of loan from any state. The opportunity that awaits you is to locate prospective borrowers in need of financing. All you need to get started are a telephone, an address, the cost of running a small classified ad, the cost of a few business cards, and, of course, affiliation with Wes-State.

This unique business can offer great financial freedom for you; it's an ideal business to operate in your spare time. You participate with Wes-State in all brokerage commissions. All you have to do is find the borrower and present the loan proposal to Wes-State. The firm finds the lender, closes the loan, and handles all the technical details.

You need no prior training, experience, or financial or business schooling. The Wes-State program will teach you everything you need to know in just a few short nights. In addition, you will receive a complete directory of lenders together with all the agreements, forms, brochures, and marketing documents you'll need for a successful loan brokerage practice.

Earnings are unlimited in the loan brokerage business. And commissions can be hefty. Loan fees of 10 percent are common. That means you can share in a $5,000 fee for placing a modest $50,000 loan.

Wes-State offers two additional programs depending on your interests and the involvement you would find most challenging. As an associate broker, you have full affiliation with Wes-State and share equally in all loan commissions. Or perhaps you have extra cash to lend on your own or know of prospective lenders? Why not join the private-lender program so you can enjoy high interest rates? We recommend participation in all three Wes-State programs, as this will provide the widest range of money-making options at little additional cost.

Whether it's the professional broker, associate broker, or private-lender program, Wes-State has a program that's right for you. Participation is between $50 and $100 depending on the program selected.

For more information, write to

Wes-State Mortgage, Inc.
834 Pearl Street
Eugene, OR   97401
(800) 356-0473

ALL-PURPOSE CLEANING CLOTH / West Coast International, Inc.

Walking through a flea market in Philadelphia, we came across a gentleman who had a large crowd positively mesmerized as he instantly made a grimy car sparkle with a few easy swipes of a cloth. We soon discovered this curious cloth was none other than "The Magical Cleaning Cloth" created by a highly secretive synthetic process and imported directly from Europe. And what a success it was! This one happy chap told us he sold 635 of these unbelievable cloths in only two days—earning more than $2,500 in profit! We knew then and there that this unbelievable magic cloth deserved a spotlight as one of our *100 Best*.

What is "The Magical Cleaning Cloth" (MCC), and what does it do?

The MCC is an unbelievable, all-purpose cleaning cloth. This synthetic chamois absorbs more water than any other cloth on the market. It is unequaled in its ability to absorb liquid spills from carpets and furniture. You can get the MCC in either heavy-duty or household size. Use the heavy-duty cloth for cars, boats, floors, dish racks, or any heavy-duty work, and the three-pack household size lighter-weight MCC for kitchen appliances, bathrooms, dishes, sinks, golf clubs, or golf balls, or to quickly put a great shine on your glassware.

Since this cloth is extremely useful in so many different ways, there is a ready market for it everywhere. This means great profits for you. The MCC is the perfect product to sell. You can sell the cloth (and related items on the brochure) through mail order, to stores, at flea markets and fairs, at parties or fund raisers, to janitorial services and main services, or directly to restaurants and bars. You can also sell directly to homes, offices, factories, or anywhere people use cleaning products. They sell fast after only a quick, easy, on-the-spot demonstration—and at a price everyone can afford.

Your prospects will instantly see the value of this "magic" cloth after watching and listening to your short demonstration. (Here's a tip. Roll two of them into a bundle and offer them for $10. People love to get a bargain and you make $8 profit out of a $10 sale.) You can make up to 500 percent profit each time.

You just cannot cover all of the sales possibilities or possibly be in dozens of places at the same time to profit from this great item. How can you get the maximum number of sales in your area? One answer is for a sales staff to work for you. You can offer good commissions on each sale and still make fabulous profits on each cloth sold. Other good money-making opportunities are to recruit organizations—churches, Scouts, Kiwanis, Lions, Rotary clubs, and so forth. Each of these groups usually wants to raise additional funds for its activities or charities, so the MCC is a natural. It is a universally needed product and gives the organization a higher-than-usual profit. Remember, there is never hard work on your part. You can have every member of any organization making money for you and themselves once you show them how wonderfully MCC works and how easily it can be sold.

MCCs are great money makers, either full- or part-time. Since they are new and not available in stores, your customers will return to you again and again when it's time to reorder. So you are assured of strong repeat business and steady income once a sales base is established.

What will it cost to earn big profits from this proven seller? Only $100 for an initial supply of The Magical Cleaning Cloth, and you're in business!

This is a great item even if you are sales-shy. West Coast International makes available a self-sell videotape demonstration of The Magical Cleaning Cloth's superpowers guaranteed to stop any crowd at a glance. If you can smile and hold your hand out for the money, you can be in business capitalizing on the secrets of MCC.

For more information, write to

West Coast International, Inc.
3912 Third Avenue
San Diego, CA   92103
(619) 297-8181
Contact: James Ziegler

MAIL-ORDER HOME-STUDY COURSE / Wilshire Mail Order Books

Did you ever have fabulous fantasies of shaking thousands of dollars from stacks of mail sent to you! Well, for some people it's no longer a fantasy. These are the shrewd entrepreneurs who mastered the science of mail-order success from one of the greatest mail-order minds of all times—Mel Powers.

Now, we know many readers of this book have a strong interest in mail order, so naturally this book wouldn't be complete unless it included Mel's widely acclaimed *Mail Order Millionaire Home Study Course.* This is *the* course in mail order. It's the very same home-study course that has turned hundreds of inexperienced entrepreneurs into mail-order success stories.

Mel specializes in self-improvement books published by his Wilshire Book Company. He has been a mail-order entrepreneur for more than 25 years, selling millions of dollars' worth of books and products. (He sold by mail order over 300,000 copies of his own *How to Get Rich in Mail Order,* which is the biggest bargain you can buy for $21.)

Armed with *Mail Order Millionaire Home Study Course,* Mel provides a firm guiding hand to ensure your mail-order success. Just a few sage pointers include

- How to find winning mail-order products
- How to get *free* display ads and publicity
- How to make big money with small classified ads
- How to make your advertising copy sizzle and make you wealthy
- How to create a best-seller using the copycat technique.

231

Packed with practical, no-nonsense advice, *Mail Order Millionaire Home Study Course* is Mel Powers' very own mail-order success strategy. Follow it and you too can become a millionaire.

This course points out a wide variety of opportunities that await you in the mail-order business, each one offering you the prospect of becoming a winner on your own terms. Study it with the proper motivation, and you will have your chance now for an exciting new career as your own boss. Best of all, you can operate your mail-order business in your spare time and still realize enormous financial success.

Mail order is a $110 billion business. But you don't have to be a Sears, Spiegel, or Montgomery Ward to cash in. More than 100,000 small mail-order companies (selling everything from books to baby clothes) are making more money than you would ever believe.

Mail Order Millionaire Home Study Course is specially priced (to readers of the *100 Best*) for only $55. As an added bonus, once you begin the course you are invited to call Mel to answer your questions and personally guide you to a more successful mail-order career!

For more information, write to

Wilshire Book Company
12015 Sherman Road
North Hollywood, CA   91605
(213) 875-1711

COMPUTER CLEANING / Your Computer Cleaning Company

Here is one previously overlooked business opportunity in the enormous world of computers with a proven service that's in great demand—cleaning the more than 20 million computers in the United States.

Just think about it. There are more than 20 million computers collecting dirt and dust—and that number will increase to 40 million in the next decade. Most of these millions have *never once been cleaned*! As boss of your very own computer cleaning company, you can be among the first to profit from this fabulous market. This is, indeed, one exploding market with virtually no competition.

Mark Winder started this exciting concept when he heard friends complain about greasy computer screens that blurred their vision or sticky keys that slowed performance. To his amazement, Mark discovered that most computer operators didn't even know they needed to clean their equipment, or they were just too busy to do it. Sensing opportunity, Mark began offering this service within local office buildings. What he found was that whether an office had 5 computers or 500, predictably its computers had never been cleaned. So an open and eager market was found! Starting part-time (while still a student), Mark quickly built his business to the point where he had six people busily working for him; he was pulling in more than $100,000 annually. Imagine what could be earned on a full-time basis!

You don't have to be a computer whiz to jump in on this opportunity. In fact, you don't need to know the first thing about running a computer to clean its exterior surfaces. With the right equipment and information, computer cleaning is simple and easy. And the results, which demonstrate the need for cleaning to even the least-observant customers, are dramatic. You can start "Your Computer Cleaning Company" part-time or full-time. That makes it a great opportunity for couples, homemakers, students, retirees—just about anyone.

Everything you need to build your own business is included in the "Your Computer Cleaning Company" kit—the equipment and materials you'll use to clean the machines and a step-by-step training video. The kit also contains your most important business tool, the "Your Computer Cleaning Company" manual—your key to building a high-profit business. This in-depth marketing and operations guidebook gives you an easy, three-step plan for finding your most productive prospects, selling your cleaning services, running your company, and making your business grow. Information-packed, it's all there, housed in a professional carrying case you'll use on the job.

When Mark started his company he commissioned a chemist to develop a unique antistatic, sanitizing fluid that easily cleans the toughest soil and grime, but with no damage to delicate plastic computer components. You'll find this exclusive solution in his kit, along with all the cleaning materials, brushes, and tools you need to do a first-rate job. And the training video takes you through the cleaning process step by step, so you can be completely confident before you handle your first cleaning job.

Mark also made the "Your Computer Cleaning Company" system remarkably easy to run. "I've taken everything I learned starting and running my own company and, with the help of two marketing professionals, developed a simple three-step plan for success," Mark claims.

This in-depth marketing and operations instruction manual will get your business growing from the very first day. It shows you how to find and reach your most productive prospects. It helps you sell your services, from your initial sales approach to the sales and operating materials you'll need to use including letters, estimate sheets, and advertising material.

The "Your Computer Cleaning Company" program is *not* a franchise. It *is* a complete business system in a kit—with a minimal capital investment. There are no franchise fees or royalties to pay, ever!

The "Your Computer Cleaning Company" kit costs just $449, plus $10 shipping and handling. You can cover the entire cost in just two days of work in your own company!

You can handle this business spending a few hours—or even less—a day. Your income can exceed $35 an hour and even more when you service large accounts with many computers. This is a repeat business and is even more ideal an opportunity if you have computer-related products or services to offer.

For more information, write to

Your Computer Cleaning Company
13229 Northrup Way, #B
Bellevue, WA   98005
(800) 232-0311, Ext. 225